■SCHOLASTIC

W9-CPC-050
Grades
1-8

THE NEXT STEP IN
Vocabulary
Instruction

Practical Strategies and Engaging Activities That Help
All Learners Build Vocabulary and Deepen Comprehension

Karen Bromley

New York • Toronto • London • Auckland • Sydney
Mexico City • New Delhi • Hong Kong • Buenos Aires

Teaching
Resources

Dedication

*With special thanks to my students and the classroom teachers
who contributed ideas to this book.*

Credits: pages 8, 75: From "Actively Engaging Middle School Students With Words." In *Best Practices in Adolescent Literacy Instruction* (Eds.) K. S. Hinchman & H. K. Sheridan-Thomas. Copyright © 2008 by the Guilford Press. Reprinted with permission of Guilford Press.

pages 22–24, 41–44, 62–64, 82–84, 102–104, 132–134: Copyright © Teaching K–8. Used by permission of Karen Bromley and www.EssentialLearningProducts.com.

pages 81, 137, 142, 144: From *Stretching Students' Vocabulary* by Karen Bromley. Copyright © 2002 by Karen Bromley. Reprinted by permission of Scholastic Inc.

Scholastic grants teachers permission to photocopy the reproducible pages from this book for classroom use. No other part of this publication may be reproduced in whole or in part, or stored in a retrieval system, or transmitted in any form or by any means, electronic, mechanical, photocopying, recording, or otherwise, without permission of the publisher. For information regarding permission, write to Scholastic Professional Books, 555 Broadway, New York, NY 10012-3999.

Cover design by Jorge J. Namerow
Interior design by Sarah Morrow
Editor: Sarah Glasscock
ISBN: 978-0-545-32114-3
Copyright © 2012 Karen Bromley
All rights reserved.
Printed in the U.S.A.

2 3 4 5 6 7 8 9 10   40   19 18 17   16 15 14 13   12

Contents

Introduction **5**

Chapter 1: Vocabulary Basics **6**
The Why of Vocabulary Instruction 6
What Affects Word Learning? 7
What Is a Word? 9
   Multiple Dimensions of a Word 11
How Are Words Learned? 11
What Concepts About Words Should Students Know? 13
Activities to Develop Students' Concepts of Words 13
   Activity: Bingo 14
   Activity: Letter Counts 14
   Activity: Word Tag 15
   Activity: Making Words With Names 15
   Activity: Making and Writing Words 16
   Activity: Synonym Names 16
   Activity: Name Acrostic 17
   Activity: Word Scrambles 17
Making Every Word a Sight Word 18
Activities to Build Students' Receptive and Expressive Vocabularies . . 19
   Activity: ASAP 19
   Activity: Badge Bingo 20
The Tricky Part—Words and Concepts 20
   Activity: Vocabulary Bookmark 21
Understanding Grammar and Language Concepts 22
Daily Calendar: Language Inquiry 22

**Chapter 2: The Role of Vocabulary
        in Comprehension and Fluency** **26**
What Is Comprehension? 26
   Comprehension Types 27
   Comprehension Connections 29
   Comprehension as Synthesis 29
   Reciprocal Comprehension 30
Wide Reading Promotes Comprehension 31
   To, With, and By Reading 31
What Is Fluency? 34
   "Just Right" Fluency 35
What Makes Words Stick? 36
   Teach Words Directly 36
      Activity: Word of the Week 37
   Provide Guided Practice 37
      Activity: Readers Theater 37

      Activity: Word Jar 38
      Activity: Word Walls 39
   Try Independent Activities 40
      Activity: World Collector 40
      Activity: Category Collector 41
      Activity: Object Collector 41
      Activity: Curiosity Collector 41
Daily Calendar: Round-the-Clock Vocabulary 41

Chapter 3: Teaching Words Well **45**
Word Consciousness 45
Aspects of Word Learning 47
Direct "Deep" Teaching 48
Knowing a Word Well 49
   Activity: "Friend or Stranger?" 49
Guidelines for Instruction 50
Offer Vocabulary-Building Activities 54
   Teach Words Directly 54
      Activity: Vocabulary Anchor 54
      Activity: K-W-L 55
      Activity: Chapter Titles 55
      Activity: 160 Words in 3 Days 56
      Activity: Flag Compare 57
      Activity: Pledge of Allegiance 57
   Provide Guided Practice 57
      Activity: Buddy Reading 58
      Activity: Journal Share 58
      Activity: Song Lyrics 58
      Activity: I Have–. Who Has—? 59
      Activity: Synonym Stretch 59
      Activity: 3-D Words 60
      Activity: Mnemonics 60
   Try Independent Activities 61
      Activity: E-Books 61
      Activity: What's New? 61
Daily Calendar: Immigration 62

Chapter 4: Looking Closely at Word Structure **65**
Word Parts and Morphology 65
Compound Words 67
   Activity: 1 + 1 = A Compound Word 68
Onsets and Rhymes 68
   Activity: Word Sorts 69

Prefixes and Suffixes 69
   Activity: Prefix Hunt 71
   Activity: Prefix "Splash" 71
   Activity: Suffix Web 71
   Activity: Earthquake 71
   Activity: Chunking 72
   Activity: Word Wheel 72
Greek and Latin Roots 73
   Activity: Divide and Conquer 74
   Activity: Greek and Latin Dictionaries 74
   Activity: Root Webs 75
   Activity: Root Trees 75
   Activity: Inspiration 76
   Activity: Word Pyramid 76
   Activity: Word Squares 77
   Activity: Flip-a-Chip 77
   Activity: Big Word Book 78
Words From Other Languages 78
Activities That Build on Similarities in Languages 78
   Activity: Writing in Two Languages 79
   Activity: Word Match 80
   Activity: Micro-Writing 80
How Does Spelling Fit? 81
   Activity: Spelling Cheerleading 81
   Try Independent Activities 81
     Activity: Sparkling Words 82
     Activity: Multisyllabic Word Hunt 82
Daily Calendar: Out of This World 82

Chapter 5: Creating Independent Word Learners **85**
There Is No "Silver Bullet" 85
Building Independence 86
   Teach Reflection 87
   Model Independence 87
   Provide Guided Practice 87
Prompts for Building Independence 88
   Prompts for Learning New or Difficult Worlds 88
   Prompts for Teaching Content-Specific Vocabulary . . . 89
Teach Content-Specific Vocabulary 90
   Six Steps 90
   Vocabulary Notebook 91
   Activity: Alphaboxes 91
   Activity: Alpha-pics 92
   Activity: 10 Important Words 93
   Activity: Word Walls 93
   Activity: ABC Books 94
   Activity: Two-Concept ABC Books 95

   Activity: Science (ELA, Social Studies, or Math) Word Sorts . . 96
Teach ELA Vocabulary 96
   Activity: Word Sort Stories 96
   Activity: Story Grammar Word Sort 98
   Activity: Word Solver 98
   Activity: 3-Word Strategy 99
   Activity: Zooming In/Zooming Out 100
   Activity: Vo-back-ulary 100
Teach Testing Vocabulary 101
   Activity: Q & A 101
Daily Calendar: Words, Words, Words 102

Chapter 6: Playing With Words **105**
Appreciating Humor 106
Ways to Play With Words 106
Wordplay Activities 108
   Teach Words Directly 108
     Activity: Wordplay and Poetry Books 108
     Activity: Writing Poetry 108
     Activity: Performance Poetry 113
     Activity: Word Ladders 113
     Activity: List Swaps .114
     Activity: Interview a Word 115
     Activity: Word Splash 116
     Activity: Quotable Quotes 117
     Activity: Chat Lingo .118
   Provide Guided Practice 119
     Activity: Sentence Tag Stories 119
     Activity: Words Are Wonderful Day 120
     Activity: Calligraphy 120
     Activity: Wikis 121
     Activity: Word Clouds 121
     Activity: Idiom Incubator 122
     Activity: Book Jackdaw 123
     Activity: Scavenger Hunt 123
   Try Independent Activities 124
     Commercial Word Games 124
     Online Word Games 126
     Activity: Unusual Words Search 128
     Activity: Alphabet Acronyms 129
     Activity: AWAD 130
     Activity: Vacation Vocabulary 130
     Activity: 10 Best Ideas for Parents 131
Daily Calendar: Chocolate. 132
Finally. 134

References **135**

Appendix: Reproducibles **137**

Introduction

Words are the keys to unlocking comprehension, fluency, and learning. This book provides word-learning strategies for classroom teachers, reading teachers, special education teachers, and teachers of English language learners (ELLs) in grades 1–8. The classroom-tested, research-based ideas you'll find here tap students' prior knowledge and engage them in listening, talking, reading, writing, and working together. But this is much more than an activity book. As you read, you will gain a better understanding of effective teaching practices and you will:

- Become a word-conscious and wise teacher of vocabulary
- Teach in ways that help students become independent word learners
- Develop the vocabulary of struggling students and ELLs
- Promote electronic and online word learning with the Internet
- Build students' enjoyment of language through lighthearted wordplay
- Use children's literature to build word knowledge and appreciation for language

In every chapter, you'll find ideas for direct instruction, guided practice, and independent activities to help all kinds of learners build rich vocabularies. In addition, questions in each chapter will help you "Extend Your Thinking" and "Teaching in Action" vignettes show you how real teachers use various vocabulary strategies. You can use many of the practices in this book (and the reproducibles in the Appendix) not only when you teach reading and writing but also when you teach science, social studies, math, and other content areas.

Karen Bromley
SUNY Distinguished Teaching Professor
Binghamton University

CHAPTER 1

Vocabulary Basics

"I'm frustrated. I give students definitions for each new word before they read, and they don't remember the words. My students can't pronounce the words when they see them in context and they don't know what the words mean when I give a vocabulary test at the end of the week."

—Kristy, a fourth-grade teacher

Like Kristy, many teachers find that students do not learn the important vocabulary they need in order to be successful readers. Some teachers use the "assign, define, and test" method, which requires students to look up words in the dictionary. Other teachers use the "identify, discuss, and assume" method, which includes defining and talking about new words. Both theory and research suggest that neither of these methods works very well. To find methods that help students learn and retain new words, we need to rethink much of the vocabulary instruction that occurs in classrooms today.

Rethinking vocabulary instruction involves asking questions. Many teachers, like Kristy, wish to become better vocabulary teachers. Here are some of their questions:

- Why is vocabulary instruction important?
- How are words learned?
- What should good vocabulary teaching look like?
- When and how often should it occur?
- How can we make word learning enjoyable and even fun for students?

This chapter answers these questions and offers several classroom-tested strategies and games for making your vocabulary teaching more effective, enjoyable, and fun.

The Why of Vocabulary Instruction

Vocabulary is one of the foundational elements of the Common Core State Standards (2011) because it is basic to listening, speaking, reading, writing, viewing, and thinking (www.corestandards.org). The K–12 standards require students to be able to do the following:

- Determine or clarify the meaning of unknown and multiple-meaning words and phrases by using context, analyzing meaningful word parts, and using references.

- Demonstrate understanding of figurative language, word relationships, and nuances in word meanings.

- Acquire and use accurately a range of general academic and domain-specific words and phrases and demonstrate independence in gathering vocabulary knowledge when encountering an unknown term important to comprehension or expression.

The ability to read complex texts and learn from content materials is also at the heart of the standards, so acquiring general vocabulary and content-specific words, as well as becoming an independent word learner, are critical to students' learning and achieving these standards.

Words are the essential building blocks of comprehension and cognition. Research shows that students who have broad vocabularies achieve better scores on classroom assessments and standardized tests than students who have limited vocabularies (Stahl & Fairbanks, 1986). Possessing rich word knowledge allows students to do the following:

- express themselves clearly

- understand what they hear and read

- have confidence when they speak

- write fluently in focused and engaging ways

- access and assess both print and digital information

- think clearly about ideas and information

- engage in the cognitive behaviors that result in learning

Mark Twain wrote, "The difference between the almost right word & the right word is really a large matter—it's the difference between the lightning bug and the lightning. A word is like a lightning bug. The *right* word is like lightning." Knowing the *right* word to use in certain situations can be critical. Consider the difference between these two sentences:

That woman is *nosey*.

That woman is *interested*.

Although the two sentences generally mean the same thing, the implied meanings differ a great deal. The first sentence has a negative connotation, while the second sentence is more neutral. Each italicized word clearly represents a specific concept or idea. Thus, words are hugely important in accurate communication, and a rich vocabulary is critical to learning and achievement.

What Affects Word Learning?

There are many factors that make word learning difficult for students (see Figure 1.1). I discuss five of these factors below. Please note that these factors are not inclusive; there is certainly overlap among them.

1. A student's *schema*, an organized collection of information that represents prior knowledge, can affect word learning.

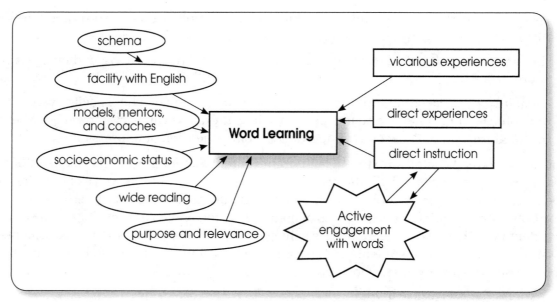

Figure 1.1 *Many factors affect word learning.*

2. A student's facility with English can affect word learning. For students whose native language is Spanish or Russian, for example, learning English may be difficult since the alphabet, sounds, graphics, and grammar of English differ from their native language. Additionally, learning English is often a slower process for a student with a delay in his or her language development or for one whose first language is not English. Having an understanding of spoken English and fluency with it promote the reading and writing of printed English. For example, knowing how to rhyme words and create word families from a phonogram and initial consonants (*-ack, back, lack, tack, snack, slack*, and so on) helps students learn more difficult words. The ability to do this indicates a growing facility with language and fluency in word learning.

3. Models, mentors, and coaches play a huge role in word learning. The books that students read or that are read to them provide excellent models for word learning. Students who read widely learn and use many more words than students who do not have access to books. This is because the written language of books is often more sophisticated than spoken language. Additionally, the kind of language that students hear from mentors and coaches (parents, teachers, friends, caregivers, and siblings) and the words these people use in conversations with students affect the amount and kind of language students use themselves. Students imitate the words and phrases they hear. Typically, a child has heard a word like *Cheerios* spoken more than once by someone before he recognizes it and uses it himself.

4. Socioeconomic status influences language development and word learning. Young children from professional homes hear approximately three million more words by the time they reach the age of three than do children from homes with fewer economic resources (Hart & Risley, 1995, p. 132). Children from poorer homes tend to have fewer experiences with words in interactions with others, learn fewer words, and acquire words more slowly than children from economically advantaged homes. For example, a child

who hears "Pick up those toys!" and a child who hears "Do you think you can pick up those toys for me now, please?" have two very different models of language to process (p. 57). The first is a command that does not require or invite a response. The second is a question that uses more words and invites cooperation and a reply. Children who have opportunities for quality interactions with parents and siblings often develop a more extensive vocabulary than children who do not have these options.

Extend Your Thinking
What impact do you believe "wide reading" has on students' word learning? What factors might affect the word learning of older students? How might you accommodate this factor in the classroom environment and in your instruction?

5. The purpose or relevance a student sees for learning words and/or language can impact how and what he or she learns. Thus, a wise teacher makes sure to explain to students why he or she is teaching certain words, how the words relate to what they already know, and what they will be able to understand or accomplish when they learn the words.

Teaching in Action

When Sean, a fifth-grade teacher, introduces a new word to his class, he knows that students may learn the word more easily if he connects it to a word they already know. For example, to teach the word fracture, *Sean connects it to* fraction. *His students know that* fraction *comes from the Latin term* fractio, *meaning "to break apart." When students connect* fracture *to* fraction, *which is part of their prior knowledge, learning and remembering the new word is easier for them. Knowing the root* fractio *can also help Sean's students figure out the meaning of related words like* infraction *and* refraction.

Then Sean explains to his students that learning the word fracture *will help them understand a newspaper article they are going to read about drilling for natural gas in their local area. He tells students that knowing the definition of* fracture *will also help them understand* fracking, *a word in the article that Sean does not intend to preteach, because he wants students to decode it on their own.*

What Is a Word?

A word can be defined as "a series of letters that go together in a special way to communicate meaning." A big part of our job is to teach new words to students not only in reading and language arts but also in science and social studies, math, health, and other subject areas. Beyond this definition, though, there are some basic things every teacher should know about words. Knowing about the following three aspects of words will help you become a better teacher of vocabulary:

- **Morphemes** are meaning units. *Example: cat* contains one morpheme—"cat"; *cats* contains two morphemes—"cat" and "s" (plural for more than one)
- **Phonemes** are sound units. *Example:* the word *a* has one phoneme or sound—"uh"; the word *the* has two phonemes—"th-uh"; *cats* has three phonemes—"kh-ah-tz."
- **Graphemes** are print units. *Example:* the letters in *cat* can be represented graphically in many ways—**cat**, **cat**, *cat*, CAT, CAT, **cat**, *CAT*

Extend Your Thinking

Some researchers believe that much of what we have seen, heard, experienced, read, or done in our lives is stored in memory. The challenge is knowing how to access or retrieve it from memory. How do you remember an important concept?

Along with the meanings, sounds, and graphics that represent a word, our brains store associations and images that connect to a word. What do you think of when you hear or see the word *cat*? I think of my tabby cat, Webster, with her white paws, bib, and soft white belly that she likes to have rubbed as she lies on her back snoozing on the carpet. The image you have may be very different. You may connect *cat* to an image in your mind of your own cat, a friend's cat, or a tiger lying under a tree in India. Or you may immediately see a cat as a machine, a caterpillar that moves dirt around.

Our brains store information linguistically and nonlinguistically (Paivio, 1990). The linguistic image is the graphic and/or phonemic representation, the word as it is printed or spoken. The nonlinguistic image might be a picture, a smell, a sound, an emotion, a feeling, and/or a memory of something related to the linguistic image. Our brains store both linguistic and nonlinguistic information about words. We call this storage *schema*. It is highly personal, as you can see from the images I just mentioned for the word *cat*. You can imagine how important this prior knowledge is in helping students make sense of the words they are learning and what they are reading.

The schema a young child has for what a word is grows with age and experiences. How do young children respond when they are asked to explain what a word is? Here are some replies that show a range of first graders' understandings:

- "A word is a sentence, a letter." (Shannon, age 5)
- "It's something like a letter. It has lots of letters put together." (Maalik, age 6)
- "Can. Can I go to the store?" (Corey, age 7)
- "Something you write in a sentence. Words are what you use out loud." (Nick, age 7)
- "Something you can spell and you can read it and if you don't know it you can skip it and go on to another word." (Clara, age 7)

Some responses show sophisticated, multidimensional understandings, while others suggest simpler, less sophisticated knowledge. For example, Shannon's definition shows inaccurate information, and Maalik's reply suggests partial understanding. Clara's answer shows us she understands how to figure out an unknown word, while Nick knows we can use words to write. Corey can even give a concrete example of what a word is, which indicates his concept of a word. So, as children grow and mature, their schema for what a word is changes and grows.

I asked these children individually to define a word, but having a class discussion of what a word is can be beneficial. As each child shares his or her definition, all students explore and extend their understandings together. If you're teaching young children, older struggling learners, or English language learners, you can use chart paper or the board to transcribe students' ideas. Then review the transcribed responses with students and use them to show students what words look like.

Multiple Dimensions of a Word

Words have similar yet varied dimensions, which is one of the reasons learning a word well is difficult for struggling students. These dimensions, or characteristics, include the following:

- **Structural:** Words consist of phonemes (sound units), morphemes (meaning units), inflectional endings (e.g., *-s, -ing, -ly*), prefixes (e.g., *un-, re-, in-, inter-*), suffixes (e.g., *-ment, -tion*), and roots (*-tract, -scope, -rupt, -port*).

- **Visual:** Words are represented graphically and can appear in different printed styles (𝗀𝗅𝗈𝖻𝖺𝗅, global, ***global***, GLOBAL) that may confuse struggling readers.

- **Grammatical:** Every word possesses a specific function in a sentence (noun, verb, adverb, adjective, and so on).

- **Semantic:** Words possess meanings and have relationships with other words (many words have multiple meanings, e.g., *hand* can mean "applause," "hand-me-down," "assistance," and so on).

- **Spoken:** Words need to be pronounced in certain standard ways or they may be misunderstood.

- **Written:** Words require proper spelling in order for a writer to communicate accurately and effectively.

How Are Words Learned?

Students learn many words through vicarious experiences (refer to the factors in Figure 1.1 on page 8). Reading the menu at a McDonald's restaurant and learning a new word is an example of vicarious learning. The young child who eats Cheerios happens to learn the word as she eats breakfast and hears her mother say, "Eat your Cheerios!" and as she sees the word *Cheerios* on the cereal box. Another example of vicarious learning is an older student who happens to learn a hyphenated word like *pro-am*, which means "professional-amateur," from the sports page or the Golf Channel. Parents who turn on the captions while they watch television give children vicarious or incidental experiences with words that build their sight vocabularies. And we know that students who read widely learn vocabulary vicariously, without instruction.

But, as Kelley, Lesaux, Kieffer, & Faller state, "Words need to be pulled apart, put together, defined informally, practiced in speech, explained in writing, and played with regularly" (2010; p. 13). This is where *direct instruction* and *guided practice* enter the vocabulary picture. Theory, research, and practical knowledge tell us that students need more than vicarious experiences to learn the large number of words necessary for them to do well in school. Students need direct instruction and guided practice in targeted words provided by a competent teacher. The competent teacher intentionally identifies and teaches words that students do not already know, words they need to know in order to understand content material, and words that will be useful to them in the future. The competent teacher also engages students in guided practice activities that involve using words together in fun, playful, and instructive ways to promote word learning. The dozens of direct instruction and guided and independent practice activities in this book will help you do that.

Teaching in Action

Chris's sixth-grade students were about to read Deborah Ellis's The Breadwinner *(Groundwood Books, 2000). Before they began to read, he first taught students the meaning and pronunciation of one of the words in the book:* burqa. *Chris used* burqa *in the following sentence and helped students infer its meaning from context: "Parvana's mother wore a burqa to cover her face when she went out in public." He also described this type of clothing worn by women in Afghanistan and showed students pictures of women wearing burqas from Google images on the Internet (he also could have used Yahoo images or flickr.com). The pictures gave students visual images and a richer understanding of the word* burqa.

Burqa could be considered a Tier 3 word. The following are definitions and examples of tier words (Beck, McKeown, & Kucan, 2002):

- **Tier 1:** Basic high-frequency words most students recognize on sight
    (e.g., *happy, baby, cat, walk*)
- **Tier 2:** Important words that appear frequently across content areas
    (e.g., *absurd, fortunate, merchant*)
- **Tier 3:** Rare, sophisticated words, and words specific to a content area
    (e.g., *albatross, peninsula, nucleus*)

Tier 2 and 3 words are more difficult than Tier 1 words, and most teachers spend more time teaching Tier 2 and 3 words than Tier 1 words. And, for this reason, they teach fewer rather than more Tier 2 and 3 words. Direct instruction in these tier words strengthens students' word learning when you do the following:

- Demonstrate how to use context: Show how pictures, words, phrases, sentences, and paragraphs surrounding an unknown word can help readers figure out the new word.

- Explore associations and connotations: Tap students' prior knowledge, background experiences, and knowledge of related words, and provide concrete and sensory images that help students learn a new word.

- Offer opportunities for repetitions: Give students multiple chances to use target words because seeing and/or hearing a word and using it several times reinforces remembering and learning a new word.

- Foster active engagement: Have students do something with the word to help make a permanent place for the new word in their schema.

To be most effective, direct instruction needs to be explicit, but it may or may not include every aspect of teaching just mentioned above. The amount and type of instruction you do for specific words will depend on the difficulty of the word(s) and the ability of your students. Some of your direct instruction will be minimal, and some of it will be extensive, but the opportunities for guided practice you provide students need to include repetitions and active engagement with words. When students participate together in games and other activities with words, they have a better chance of learning, remembering, and using those words later.

Of course, helping students become independent word learners as a result of your instruction should be your overriding goal. One way to foster comprehension and build independence is to help students begin to use fix-up strategies to figure out unknown words on their own (see Figure 1.2). This list of strategies was created by fourth-grade students and shows the most helpful ways to attack hard words. Later chapters will include more discussion of direct instruction, guided practice, and building independence.

Fix-Up Strategies

☺ Think what makes sense.

✍ Look at the picture.

↩ Read it again.

– → Skip it and read on.

💡 Think about words I know.

👄 Get my mouth ready.

c[a]t Look for a chunk & frame it.

ᵃbᶜ Sound it out.

? Ask for help.

Extend Your Thinking

How might you simplify and/or reword these fix-up strategies for first- or second-grade students? How could you use pictures to help you do this?

Figure 1.2 *Teach these fix-up strategies to students to help them figure out difficult words.*

What Concepts About Words Should Students Know?

Many children seem to acquire knowledge about printed words intuitively as they realize that what they say can be written down. Other students need help in building understandings about words that are key to becoming successful readers, writers, and communicators. Conversations with both young children and older students should include the following notions:

- A word means something.
- A word can mean different things.
- Your name is a word.
- A word is made up of letters.
- The letters in a word stay near each other.
- You can say and write a word.

It is important to determine whether struggling readers and English language learners possess these concepts about words. So, ask individuals or students in small groups to show you a letter, a word, a sentence, and a paragraph to assess their understanding of these concepts. Then teach them the basic knowledge they need to acquire vocabulary and become literate.

Activities to Develop Students' Concept of Word

These activities help students understand that words are composed of letters that go together in certain ways. Each activity initially requires direct instruction before students move to guided practice.

ACTIVITIES ![] **Bingo**

Materials: index cards, marker, tokens (cereal pieces or chips), bingo card

Name Bingo: This activity focuses students' attention on the structure of familiar words.

Teaching in Action

Nicki, a first-grade teacher, prints each letter of a child's name on an index card, mixes up the cards, and then has each child arrange the letters in the correct order on a desk or other flat surface. As Nicki randomly calls out letters and writes them on the board, children place a chip on a card when that letter in their name is called. When all the letters in a child's name are covered, the child says "bingo" and then he or she helps a neighbor until everyone's letters are covered and everyone has declared "bingo." So everyone "wins" in this game.

Word Bingo: Play a different kind of bingo game with students. In this form of bingo, create two or three different sets of bingo cards with a different word in each of nine boxes and read aloud the definitions for words, one at a time. Students must find the correct word and draw an X through it. When someone has three words in a row or diagonally, they say "bingo!" (Use fewer or more than nine boxes/words depending on the age or ability of your students.)

ACTIVITY ![] **Letter Counts**

Materials: 5-inch by 8-inch index cards, markers, poster board

This activity gives students practice in recognizing and pronouncing each other's names, counting, and reading bar graphs.

Teaching in Action

Nicki writes each first-grader's name on a 5-inch by 8-inch index card. She has children count the letters and write that numeral on the card. Then Nicki creates a bar graph poster of names containing the same number of letters and displays it on a classroom bulletin board. During free time, pairs of children use a pointer to practice pronouncing classmates' names and talk about what the poster shows.

ACTIVITY ■ Word Tag

This game sensitizes students to how words sound in order to help them see how letters go together to make words and how rearranging letters can make new words.

Teaching in Action

In her second-grade classroom, Jamie builds facility and fluency with English by having students listen for the final sound in a word and then supplying a word that begins with that sound. She starts the game by saying a word and then inviting a student to say a new word that begins with the last letter or sound of that word.

Jaime: *I'll begin Word Tag with the word* pencil. *Who can tag onto my word with a word that begins with "l"?*

Student 1: *The word* light *begins with "l." Who can tag onto my word with a word that begins with "t"?*

Student 2: *The word* telephone *begins with "t." Who can tag onto my word with a word that begins with "e"?*

ACTIVITY ■ Making Words With Names

Materials: Andy, That's My Name *by Tomie DePaola (Aladdin, 1999), paper, index cards, markers*

This game gives children opportunities to explore putting letters together to make new words, and it builds sight vocabulary and spelling knowledge.

Richard	Alison	Karen
Rich	Al	are
hard	is	ear
card	on	near
rid	son	rake
hair	lion	ran
chair	sin	
arch	lain	
	ail	

Figure 1.3 *Arranging and rearranging the letters in their names helps students learn how to make words.*

Teaching in Action

Andy, That's My Name *by Tomie DePaola shows how the letters in "Andy" can be rearranged to form new words. Before reading the book aloud to her second graders, Jaime chooses a child's name that contains two vowels and makes a list of possible words that can be made from the name. She'll use this to model how to play the Making Words With Names game (Cunningham & Allington, 2011). Then Jaime prints the letters of each child's name on separate index cards. She prints vowels in red and underlines each letter so children can align the letters correctly and not mistake a "p" for a "d," for example. After reading aloud the book and modeling the game, Jaime has children rearrange their letter cards to form new words and share them orally with the class. Figure 1.3 shows examples using three children's names.*

This activity also helps older students build their awareness of how letters go together to form words. To begin, have students use the letters of their first names and then transition to seasonal or content vocabulary, for example, *Thanksgiving, hurricane, spider,* or *revolution.* Older students often enjoy this challenge, and pairing struggling students with more capable students can make it more enjoyable for everyone. (Do you realize that students can make nearly 100 new words from a word such as *planets*?)

ACTIVITY ■ # Making and Writing Words

Materials: index cards, markers, directions, and game sheet in Figure 1.4

Rasinski & Padak (2007) developed this slightly more advanced version of the Making Words With Names game. It provides an opportunity for students in grade 2 and up to write words they create from a number of vowels and consonants you provide. It promotes spelling and aids students' ability to remember words.

MAKING WORDS WITH NAMES GAME

- Choose a secret word (such as *revolution*).
- Identify the smaller words you can make from the letters in the secret word and think of a clue that will help students identify it (for example, "This three-letter word means the opposite of *in*"), as well as the sequence of the clues. *Note:* Keep the last box blank.
- Create a game sheet like the one shown below and distribute a sheet to each student.

Vowels		Consonants	
1	7	13	
2	8	14	
3	9	15	
4	10	16	
5	11	17	
6	12	18	

- Share a clue for each smaller word you identified, for example, "This three-letter word means the opposite of *in*. Write this word in box 1." Continue until you have given all the clues.
- Then challenge students to decipher the secret word by putting together the letters in the smaller words.
- Finally, use the secret word to launch a story or a class discussion of the word.

Figure 1.4 *Making and Writing Words*

ACTIVITY ■ # Synonym Names

Materials: dictionary, 5-inch by 8-inch index cards, markers

In this activity students use the dictionary to find words that describe themselves and that begin with the initials of their first and last names.

Teaching in Action

Bruce has his fourth-grade students find two descriptive adjectives: The first adjective must begin with the initial of their first name, and the second adjective must begin with the initial of their last name.

Examples: Curious Brainy, Carmel Blackman—Amusing Fascinating, Alan French.

Students write their "new" names on an index card and Bruce posts them on a bulletin board. Bruce says that some of these descriptive words even turn up in students' writing.

ACTIVITY ▪ Name Acrostic

Materials: dictionary, index cards, markers

Students use the dictionary to find descriptive multisyllabic words for an acrostic.

Teaching in Action

Bruce asked his fourth graders to search for multisyllabic words to describe themselves. Their acrostic would use each letter in their first name. Karen wrote this acrostic:

> *K*nowledgeable
>
> *A*wesome
>
> *R*unner
>
> *E*nergetic
>
> *N*ervous

Bruce also uses this exercise in social studies by having his students create a descriptive acrostic for a person, concept, or location from a topic they are studying. The acrostic that Matt created for the Cheyenne tribe of Native Americans shows some of the information he learned during his study of these people (see Figure 1.5).

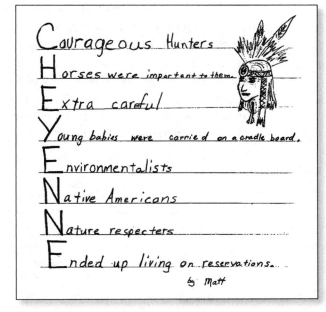

Figure 1.5 *Students can use vocabulary and content knowledge to create an acrostic.*

ACTIVITY ▪ Word Scrambles

Materials: handheld devices with vocabulary applications

Older students who own handheld devices like Droids or iPhones can download a number of free applications (apps) to improve their vocabularies. For instance, the *Word Warp* and the *Word Popper* applications give a player several letters, and then time the player as he or she rearranges letters to create as many words as possible. Longer words receive more points than shorter words. Two other app games, *Words With Friends* and *Scramble: Challenge Editions*, are played online in similar fashion, but they differ in one respect: They can be played with friends or other players subscribing to a social networking site. The games give immediate reinforcement when players spell words correctly, but they do not give credit for nonwords or incorrect spelling.

So, for students who enjoy technology and have access to it, learning what a word is and vocabulary building can happen electronically. Games like these are challenging and allow players to compete with themselves and others to grow their vocabularies.

In addition to helping students develop the concept of what a word is, the last three activities—Synonym Names, Name Acrostic, and Word Scrambles—expand students' vocabularies and encourage the use of the dictionary, an element of the Common Core State Standards (2011).

Making Every Word a Sight Word

Good vocabulary instruction ensures that words become part of students' *receptive* and *expressive* vocabularies. The receptive vocabulary contains all the words a student understands when he or she listens and reads. The expressive vocabulary holds all the words a student uses when he or she speaks and writes. It is not enough for students to understand the meaning of a word when it is spoken or as they read it in print. But, for most students, understanding spoken words is the step that precedes reading words in print. Both these receptive activities, listening and reading, are preliminary to using words in speaking and writing. To really know and use a word well, the word should be part of students' receptive and expressive vocabularies. Vicarious experiences and direct experiences often do not allow words to become part of both receptive and expressive vocabularies. But, when you provide good direct instruction and plenty of opportunities for guided practice, you help students really know and use words well.

Receptive Vocabulary	Expressive Vocabulary
Listening	Speaking
Reading/Viewing	Writing/Composing

Two terms often used in discussions of vocabulary are *sight* and *meaning*. Sight words refer to all the words a reader recognizes immediately and can read when he or she sees them. Examples of sight words for a young child are *a, the, an, and, can, was, saw, they, them,* and *who.* A meaning vocabulary consists of all the words a reader might be able to define if given a chance to decode the word and/or see it in the context of a sentence or paragraph. A typical young child's meaning vocabulary contains words such as *birthday, elephant,* and *pancake.* When a word like *birthday* is part of a child's sight and meaning vocabulary, the child recognizes the word and knows its meaning when he or she reads it in print. *Birthday* becomes part of his or her receptive vocabulary when the child recognizes it in print and when it is spoken. *Birthday* becomes part of his or her expressive vocabulary when the child can both say it and use it appropriately in writing.

Ideally, your goal should be to increase students' sight vocabularies to the point that they recognize and understand instantly nearly every word they meet; for example, words in a fourth grader's meaning vocabulary might be *temperature, democracy, mummy,* and *geography.* These may not yet be sight words for some students, who might hesitate when reading them and need to decode or use context to figure out their meanings and pronounce them. But, once a student meets words like these several times, he or she will become familiar with them and recognize them on sight. Our goal is to have a marriage between the sight and meaning vocabularies of students. Think about your own reading of this text. Your sight and meaning vocabularies have blended over time. Almost every word you come to as you read, you recognize immediately. You know the meaning for that word and can pronounce it, and hopefully you can use it when you talk and write.

Activities to Build Students' Receptive and Expressive Vocabularies

ACTIVITY ■ **ASAP (As Soon As Possible)**

Materials: 3-inch by 5-inch index cards (two different colors), marker

In this game, partners try to give answers as quickly as they can, which gives students the opportunity to build sight and meaning vocabularies simultaneously.

Write each letter of the alphabet individually on index cards of one color and write categories of things (e.g., bird, fruit, plant, *or* something to do in summer, something crunchy, and so on) on another set of index cards of another color (see Figure 1.6). Have partners take turns picking a letter card and a category card and supplying an appropriate word that begins with the letter. Students can also write their words and keep lists of them (see Figure 1.7). This game causes students to recognize printed category words and tap their prior knowledge to supply verbal examples of words that fit the category.

Figure 1.6 *ASAP builds spoken vocabulary.*

bird	country	*something to do in summer*	*something that swims*
fruit	adverb	*something crunchy*	*something made with chocolate*
plant	adjective	*something sticky*	*something sharp*
month	noun	*something sweet*	*something that is a gas*
sound	wild animal	*something rough*	*something wet*
number	meat	*something in a cafeteria*	*something found in a gym*
pet's name	ice cream flavor	*something that comes in pairs*	*something salty*
verb	river	*something warm*	*something that is a liquid*
city	vegetable	*something to do in a city*	*something black*
girl's name	boy's name	*something cold*	*something in the classroom*
state	candy	*something in the refrigerator*	*something on a farm*
sport	flower	*something with wings*	*something sour*

Figure 1.7 *ASAP also builds written vocabulary.*

ACTIVITY ■ **Badge Bingo**

Materials: a book or a chapter students have just read, paper and markers, scissors, a plastic name badge for each student

Play this game with students to reinforce important vocabulary and meanings.

BADGE BINGO GAME

1. Select words that are important to review with students and for them to know from a book or a chapter they have just read. Choose one word for each student in your class or group.

2. Create a table that has a square for each word you selected and write a word in each square. Make a copy for each student and one copy to cut apart.

3. Then create another table that has a square for each word you selected and write the definition of each word in a square. You can do this easily on the computer or by hand.

4. Cut out the words and definitions and put them in a plastic name badge. The word should face out, and its definition should face the student.

5. Give a badge to each student. Make sure students wear their badges with the word facing out. Also distribute the sheet of words you made in Step 2 to each student.

6. Tell students to circulate and to pair up with their classmates, one at a time, to define the words they see on their classmates' badges. (The definitions on the back of the badge help the badge wearer know if a classmate's definition is correct.)

7. When a student defines a word correctly, the badge wearer initials that student's word sheet. Play continues until everyone's sheet is filled or one student has a full sheet.

Teaching in Action

Sandra taught Badge Bingo to a group of fourth-grade students who had just finished reading and discussing the book Hoot *by Carl Hiassen (2004). Sandra identified 15 important words from the story—one for each student in the group—and they played the game until all students had defined all the words and had initials in every box on their sheet (see Figure 1.8). This game gets students moving around the classroom as they add words to their sight vocabularies and provide meanings for words.*

owl	hoot	deforestation
renegade	sinister	intrigue
mumble	crocodile	hastily
permit	perch	mullet
mercury	criminals	law

Figure 1.8 *words from* Hoot

The Tricky Part—Words and Concepts

Words are a combination of sounds and/or letters that are labels for things, feelings, emotions, ideas, and concepts. It is easier to teach a struggling third-grade writer who uses incomplete sentences but can distinguish between nouns and verbs how to share a message with clarity. It is easier to teach subtraction and addition to second-grade students who struggle with math but who know the meaning of the words *less* and *more*. On the other hand, not knowing a word like *democracy* can make it difficult for fifth-grade students to understand words like *constitution* and *freedom*.

 The Next Step in Vocabulary Instruction © 2012 by Karen Bromley, Scholastic Teaching Resources

How are words different from concepts? Are *noun*, *less*, and *democracy* words or concepts? Janelle, a fifth-grade teacher, explains the difference to her students.

Teaching in Action

Janelle tells her students, "Think like an astronomer. Think of a word as a star and a concept as a constellation. The difference between them is a matter of magnitude, with many stars making up a constellation. For example, the North Star and other stars make up the constellation we call the Big Dipper." (See Figure 1.9.)

Then Janelle gets more specific. She says, "Let me give you some examples. Noun is a word that represents a concept because it has a broad meaning with a variety of possibilities: nouns are words for people, places, things, or ideas. Less is a word, not a concept, since it has a meaning with a narrow scope: it means 'without or not as much as.' And, finally, democracy is a word that represents a concept because it has a broad meaning that includes other words, such as constitution, freedom, equality, emancipation, justice, capitalism, and so on.

- *Word*—series of speech sounds or printed characters that represent meaning
- *Concept*—idea or construct

Think like an astronomer!

Word—a star

Concept—a constellation

Figure 1.9 *Think of words as stars and concepts as constellations.*

How does this distinction affect Janelle's teaching? Understanding the narrow and broad aspects of words allows her to make decisions about whether, how, and when to teach vocabulary. Helping her students recognize, understand, and appropriately use the word *less* is easier than helping them recognize, understand, and appropriately use the word *democracy*. Janelle believes that the meanings of some words may be clear from the context in which they are used, and so they aren't worth teaching; however, before her students read, she believes in spending time teaching them words that represent difficult concepts and whose meaning cannot be inferred from context. She also reviews those difficult words after students have finished reading. She reports, "I find it helps students remember those words."

Occasionally, Janelle opts not to teach new concepts before reading. She says, "I like to give students the opportunity to use their own word-attack skills to figure out unknown words." In these cases, Janelle uses the Vocabulary Bookmark activity below. Then she does word work after students finish reading to make sure everyone understands those difficult concepts that they have identified.

ACTIVITY ■ Vocabulary Bookmark

Materials: paper, marker, scissors, sticky notes

Give each student a vocabulary bookmark and have everyone write new, difficult, or interesting words (and the page numbers where they appear in the text) for discussion after reading. You can also let students use sticky notes. (See sample Vocabulary Bookmark template in Figure 1.10.)

Vocabulary Bookmark

Interesting or Unknown Words I Found

Name:

Book I am Reading:

New or unusual words I discovered:

Word   Page No.

Figure 1.10 *Students can identify difficult words with this Vocabulary Bookmark as they read.*

Understanding Grammar and Language Concepts

It's important for students to know why we are teaching them certain things and why we are teaching in a particular way. If students understand why we are doing something, then they are more likely to adopt a purpose for doing it and to be successful. Knowing the vocabulary of grammar is important because it helps students in their writing. For example, students who have the necessary vocabulary can talk about their own writing and more easily revise it for clarity.

See page 25 for a list of great grammar books to share with students.

Teaching in Action

Before Janelle does a grammar lesson on possessives, which her fifth graders are shaky on, they explore the concept of possessives, including the terms apostrophe, singular, *and* plural. *She explains to students how mastering possessives will make them good writers who communicate effectively with their audience. Janelle explains, "When students know why they are learning something, it becomes relevant for them and they more often buy into participating."*

Daily Calendar: Language Inquiry

The Daily Calendar is an effective way to reinforce a range of language skills with your students. The activities in the calendar help students learn about the many ways in which people and animals use language to communicate. The activities are appropriate for differentiating instruction for a range of ability levels. They can be used with a whole class, small groups, or individuals for targeted instruction or enrichment, or sent home as homework for parental/sibling involvement. If families do not have Internet access, they may be able to use the computers at their public library to do the activities on the list.

DAILY CALENDAR: LANGUAGE INQUIRY

Week 1: Getting Started

1. **Have your class** look up the words *language* and *communication* on Wikipedia (www.wikipedia.com) or a classroom dictionary to find their definitions. Make a list of all the different languages and second languages spoken in your classroom. Make a list of all the ways we communicate.

2. **Ask students** to survey families, friends, and neighbors about the languages they speak and their countries of origin. Add these to the classroom list you created on Day 1. Talk about why many different spoken languages exist and what language does for a culture.

3. **Locate on a map** each country identified yesterday. Find the closest Native American tribes to you and identify their native language. Show students where Spanish, French, and English are primarily spoken in North America (Mexico, Quebec, and the remainder of Canada and the United States, respectively).

4. **Use a search engine** such as Google or Bing to search the term "cave drawings." Visit www.culture.gouv.fr/culture/arcnat/lascaux/en to see pictures from the Cave of Lascaux in France and talk with students about the roles of storytelling and cave art in early cultures.

 The Next Step in Vocabulary Instruction © 2012 by Karen Bromley, Scholastic Teaching Resources

5. **Encourage your class** to create beautiful cave drawings with markers and chalk on butcher paper and then have students share the stories their pictures represent with one another.

Week 2: Moving On

6. **For homework,** have students find out what the words *petroglyph* and *pictograph* mean. First, help them discover meanings that morphemes provide (*petro* = rock, *picto* = picture, *graph* = write or draw, and *glyph* = carve). You can find these by searching "Greek and Latin roots" on the Web.

7. **Read *The Riddle of the Rosetta Stone*** by James Cross Giblin (Crowell, 1990) to your students. Help them learn about the ancient Egyptian writing called hieroglyphics and how scientists broke the code of the Rosetta Stone.

8. **Visit the Gutenberg Web site** (www.gutenberg.de/english/erfindun.htm) with your students to help them learn about the invention of the printing press and the impact it had on the world.

9. **Ask your school's art teacher** to do woodblock printing or potato printing with your students to give them a sense of what the original printing process was all about.

10. **Find out** about the languages spoken by early Native American people, the meaning of smoke signals, and Universal Indian Sign Language when you and your students visit www.inquiry.net/outdoor/native/sign/smoke-signal.htm.

Week 3: Poetry, Art, and Music

11. **Discover the language** of art. Before reading aloud *The Stinky Cheese Man* by Jon Scieszka (Viking, 1992), look at the pictures and discuss the messages they communicate. Then read the story to see how the text reflects the pictures.

12. **Compare the artwork** in *The Stinky Cheese Man* with the artwork in *A River Ran Wild* (Harcourt, 1992) or another of Lynne Cherry's books. Look at Cherry's pictures first to see what messages they convey, then read the text. Compare Cherry's realism with the surrealism and fantasy in Lane Smith's work.

13. **Learn about rap** and its origins by reading *The History of Rap Music* by Cookie Lommell (Chelsea House, 2001). Introduce students to rap with *M.C. Turtle and the Hip Hop Hare* by David Vozar (Doubleday, 1995), a rap retelling of Aesop's fable.

14. **Write rap** with your students. First, read a book like *Fables* by Arnold Lobel (HarperCollins, 1983) and then have the class choose a favorite story to rewrite in rap form. Then students can form small groups to write their own raps and share them with the class.

15. **Read poetry** by Shel Silverstein, such as *A Light in the Attic* (Evil Eye Music, 1981), and share his simple ink illustrations with students. These short, humorous poems are about everyday things. Brainstorm a list of topics to write about and have students write and illustrate their own poems.

16. **Ask your school's music teacher** to teach a lesson on the language of music and how different instruments in an orchestra communicate various moods and feelings depending on sound, tone, meter, and timbre.

17. **Play the Making Words game** (see page 15) using the word *communicate*, with students working in pairs to rearrange the letters into as many smaller words as they can. (They should be able to make at least 20 words.)

18. **Learn about Net lingo.** Ask students if they know about instant messaging, or IM. Go to www.webopedia. com/quick_ref/textmessageabbreviations.asp for a dictionary of IM terms, such as LOL (laugh out loud); TTYL (talk to you later); and NP (no problem). See how many your students know.

19. **Pair students** and invite them to write notes to each other using the IM terms they have learned. After they have created their note, have them swap and then translate the IM terms into standard English.

Week 4: Extend Yourself

20. **Teach students Pig Latin** (ig-pay atin-lay). On the board, show how syllables are turned around in Pig Latin and model the sound of it by offering a few oral examples of your own. Pair students so they can use Pig Latin with each other. Talk about why different languages and forms of language have developed.

21. **Read** *The Whales' Song* by Dyan Sheldon (Penguin, 199), *Whales Passing* by Eve Bunting (Scholastic, 2003), or another story about the language of whales. Discuss how and why nonhuman animals communicate.

22. **Visit** www.cs.ucf.edu/~MidLink/whale.html to see pictures of whales and dolphins and to learn about how these animals make the sounds that allow them to communicate.

23. **Hear the language** of the bottlenose whale, sperm whale, bottlenose dolphin, and others at http://neptune. atlantis-intl.com/dolphins/sounds.html. Find out why sounds and hearing are so important for these animals.

24. **Brainstorm** and list the slang words your students currently use. Make a list of slang terms that are no longer "in" and talk about why and how English changes. Share some of the slang you used when you were younger.

25. **Invite a local radio or television personality** to visit. Beforehand, brainstorm a list of language and questions to ask this person about his or her job. Afterward, send your visitor a class thank-you note.

Week 5: More About Language

26. **Invite your school's speech teacher** to talk to your students about how humans create and receive sounds. Ask him or her to teach students some tongue twisters!

27. **Teach students** to finger spell. Find an animated American Sign Language (ASL) finger-spelling alphabet at http://library.thinkquest.org/J002137/abc.html. Talk about how this language developed to help people communicate.

28. **Invite your school's ELL teacher** to talk about the difficulties faced by speakers of other languages as they learn English. Be sure to focus on how ELL speakers enrich our classrooms and talk about what they can teach English speakers and vice versa.

29. **Have students** use collage art materials to make pictures representing the many meanings of the term *language*, and have them give each picture a title. Share pictures in small groups and post them on a bulletin board or outside your classroom.

30. **Plan an open-mike session** in which students take turns reading an original poem or story about what they have learned about language in the past month. Allow students to practice first using a microphone, then invite parents or another class to be the audience.

BOOKS ABOUT GRAMMAR

These children's books do a terrific job of teaching students the grammar-related words that can help them be better readers and writers.

- *Punctuation Celebration* by Elsa Knight Bruno (Henry Holt, 2009) (Grades 2–6). Written in rhyme, this book explains to young writers how and when to use different punctuation marks. Each punctuation mark includes a poem written to demonstrate its correct use.

- *Greedy Apostrophe: A Cautionary Tale* by Jan Carr (Holiday House, 2007) (Grades 1–4). In this book, the apostrophe goes all over town inserting himself in places where he does not belong and causes much confusion while showing students how not to use the apostrophe.

- *Merry-Go-Round: A Book About Nouns* by Ruth Heller (Grosset & Dunlap, 1990) (Grades 1–4). With colorful illustrations, this book teaches readers all about nouns, including common, proper, abstract, concrete, compound, singular, plural, and possessive nouns. Heller has also written other books on the parts of speech including *Many Luscious Lollipops: A Book about Adjectives* (1998); *Kites Sail High: A Book About Verbs* (1998); *Up, Up and Away: A Book About Adverbs* (1998); *Behind the Mask: A Book About Prepositions* (1998); *Fantastic! Wow! and Unreal!: A Book About Interjections and Conjunctions* (2000); and *Mine! All Mine! A Book About Pronouns* (1999).

- *Punctuation Takes a Vacation* by Robin Pulver (Holiday House, 2003) (Grades 1–6). When all the punctuation marks in Mr. Wright's class decide to take a vacation, the students discover just how difficult life can be without them. Students can add appropriate punctuation to postcards that come to the class having no punctuation.

- *Nouns and Verbs Have a Field Day* by Robin Pulver (Holiday House, 2006) (Grades 1–4). The children in Mr. Wright's class take a field day while nouns and verbs have fun of their own showing students the roles of these two parts of speech.

- *Silent Letters Loud and Clear* by Robin Pulver (Holiday House, 2008) (Grades 1–4). Mr. Wright's students express a dislike for silent letters and the offended letters decide to go on strike to teach them a lesson. Silent letters are shown in color or with a caret (^) so the reader can see how words look without the letter.

- *Eats, Shoots & Leaves: Why, Commas Really Do Make a Difference!* by Lynne Truss (Putnam, 2006) (Grades 1–4). If you are tired of explaining and re-explaining the importance of punctuation in writing, then this is the book for you. There is a version for older students, too.

- *The Girl's Like Spaghetti: Why, You Can't Manage Without Apostrophes!* by Lynne Truss (Putnam, 2007) (Grades 2–5) "Eat here, and get gas!" or "Eat here and get gas." Students will gain an instinctive understanding of the traffic signals of language as they learn about apostrophes, commas, periods, and exclamation points.

- *The War Between the Vowels and the Consonants* by Priscilla Turner (Farrar, Straus & Giroux, 1999) (Grades 1–3). The mutual irritation between vowels and consonants escalates into war in this tale, which fosters thinking about how letters work together to make words and how people live together in peace.

- *Word Builder* by Ann Whitford Paul (Simon & Schuster, 2009) (Grades 1–3). This book introduces words, sentences, punctuation, paragraphs, chapters, and other vocabulary of writing. The text is limited and uses poetry and images.

Although I have included the publishers' recommended grade levels for these books, each book works well with older students. The same is true for many children's books typically thought of as being for younger students. The books listed here simplify difficult concepts and are effective with students of all levels.

CHAPTER 2

The Role of Vocabulary in Comprehension and Fluency

"I learned in biology class a few years ago that our bodies are composed of over 60 percent water. I like to think of my body makeup as a metaphor for the relationships among vocabulary, comprehension, and fluency. Vocabulary is the water. Comprehension is my skeleton, and fluency is my muscle. Vocabulary (water) is basic to both comprehension (my bones) and fluency (my muscles)."

—Tanya, a sixth-grade teacher

Tanya uses this metaphor to help her students link word learning to understanding what they read and to read easily with appropriate stress and expression. It alerts Tanya's students to the key role words play in reading comprehension and oral reading fluency.

What Is Comprehension?

Comprehension allows us to understand and enjoy text. Pronouncing words correctly and reading with fluency are good skills to possess, but understanding what we read is the real purpose for reading. To promote comprehension, we first have to recognize the significant role vocabulary plays in comprehension. By some estimates, vocabulary comprises as much as 70–80 percent of comprehension (Nagy & Scott, 2000). Knowing the meaning of a word, besides knowing how to pronounce it, is basic to understanding the sentence, paragraph, or selection where the word appears.

Struggling readers often exhibit limited comprehension and fluency, and lack vocabulary and concept knowledge for the following reasons:

- They have little content-specific prior knowledge.
- They have limited exposure to rich language and lack interest in language.
- They lack knowledge of how to use context to learn new words.
- They have difficulty decoding multisyllabic words.
- They lack knowledge of inflectional endings, prefixes, suffixes, and roots.
- Their first language is not English.
- They avoid reading as an independent activity.

For these reasons, building the vocabularies of struggling readers is one of the most daunting tasks and important responsibilities you have as a teacher. But understanding how vocabulary affects comprehension and fluency is critical for teaching all students, not just struggling readers. Many teachers rely on the following models, or some combination of them, in their classrooms to link vocabulary and comprehension:

- Comprehension types
- Comprehension connections
- Comprehension as synthesis
- Reciprocal comprehension

Comprehension Types

Like vocabulary, comprehension is a foundational element of the Common Core State Standards (2011). The standards specifically aim for students at all grade levels to "expand their vocabulary in the course of studying content" and to be proficient at reading and understanding complex nonfiction texts.

There is a variety of ways to think about the comprehension of complex text. In one model, comprehension consists of literal, interpretive, and applied understandings. This model is popular because of its simplicity.

- *Literal* comprehension is understanding what is right there in a picture or in print on the page or screen. This kind of comprehension involves "reading the lines" or understanding what is actually written on the page.

- *Interpretive* comprehension involves understanding what comes from "reading between the lines." In other words, when we interpret what an author has created or written, we use some of our own knowledge along with what we read and weave both together to understand the author's message.

- *Applied* comprehension is understanding that comes from "reading beyond the lines." Students who possess applied comprehension connect what they read to situations beyond or outside the print or picture. Interpretive and applied comprehension are sometimes characterized as deep, rich, or thoughtful reading comprehension.

To see how this model of comprehension might work, look at the questions that Terry, a fourth-grade teacher, posed to his class about a passage on bald eagles to supplement the science unit he was teaching (see Figure 2.1).

Terry uses QAR (Question Answer Relationships) (Raphael, 1986) to help his students rely on different information sources to answer questions: *In the Book QARs* (Right There, Think and Search) and *In My Head QARs* (On My Own, Author and Me). After his students read the passage, Terry asks them to respond in writing to the types of QARs to determine their comprehension. Notice how the QARs align with the literal, interpretive, and applied model discussed earlier.

Literal (or *Right There QAR*):

- Where are bald eagles found?
- What size nest do bald eagles build?

THE BALD EAGLE

Although eagles have been removed from the Endangered Species List, the bald eagle is still protected under the federal government's Migratory Bird Act. The bald eagle is a migratory bird of prey and the national bird and symbol of the United States. Bald eagles live near large bodies of open water with an abundant food supply and old-growth trees for nesting. The bald eagle builds the largest nest of any North American bird, up to 13 feet deep, 8 feet wide, and 1 ton in weight. The bald eagle is not actually bald. Its name derives from an older meaning of the word, which means "white headed." The diet of these birds consists mainly of fish, but they are opportunistic feeders. They hunt by swooping down and snatching fish out of the water with their talons. Or a bald eagle may wait for other birds of prey to catch food and then snatch the food away from them. In the wild, the bald eagle can live up to 30 years, and it often survives longer in captivity. Today, besides the bald eagle, there are 58 other eagle species in the world.

Figure 2.1

Interpretive (or *Think and Search QAR*):

- What do you think *opportunistic* means here?
- How many different kinds of eagle species are there in the world today?
- What does *old-growth forests* mean here?

Applied (or *Author and Me QAR*):

- Why do you think bald eagles have been removed from the endangered list?
- Why do you think we chose the bald eagle as our national symbol?

Vocabulary is important to comprehending this passage. If students did not know the meanings of the words *migratory, endangered, abundant, symbol, opportunistic, old-growth,* and *captivity,* they likely had a difficult time comprehending the passage. Terry assumed that context would aid his students in figuring out many of these words. And, since he wanted students to use their own word-attack skills, he chose not to preteach any vocabulary.

However, notice the way Terry asked his students for the meanings of two terms used in the passage (*opportunistic* and *old-growth*): He asks them what the terms "mean here." Often, students can supply the meaning of a word, but not in the sense that it is being used in the text. For example, a student might define *opportunistic* as "taking a chance" or "making use of an opportunity." Both definitions are correct, but neither defines the word as it's used in the passage, so Terry tells his students to define *opportunistic* and *old-growth* forests as they relate specifically to the passage. Students can infer the meanings of both these terms by reading between the lines: bald eagles are opportunistic because they steal food other birds have caught. This straightforward way of categorizing comprehension into three levels may help struggling students focus on the print and read it carefully. One drawback of this approach is that it does not always take into account students' prior knowledge.

Extend Your Thinking

Do you think written answers to the questions about the bald eagle passage would be a valid measure of students' comprehension? Why or why not?

Comprehension Connections

Another strategy is to have students think of comprehension as connections. In *Mosaic of Thought* (2007), Keene and Zimmerman describe this model as one where teachers ask students to make *connections to self, connections to text(s)*, and *connections to the world*. Here are some connections that students might make that demonstrate their comprehension of the passage in Figure 2.1:

- **Connections to self:** "We have a bald eagle nest on a telephone pole near our house. It's huge and it's made of sticks." (Jason)

- **Connections to text(s):** "Remember when we read *There's an Owl in the Shower* by Jean Craighead George? We learned all about the spotted owl of the Pacific Northwest that was endangered." (Madeleine)

- **Connections to the world:** "I think it's all the pollution and chemicals we put into our environment that make the egg shells soft. Then the hatchlings never hatch and can't grow up. I saw a show on TV that said this is why they became extinct." (Cody)

When a teacher uses connections to promote understanding, many different answers can be appropriate depending on a student's prior knowledge. When a teacher uses literal, interpretive, and applied comprehension questions, students may rely less on their own prior knowledge and more on the text and interpreting it. To answer literal and interpretive questions, information has to come from the print. Only applied questions require the use of prior knowledge. Jackie, a fourth-grade teacher, says, "Asking students connections questions allows for individuality in responses. Asking students 'to connect' encourages their personal engagement with text. Because the connections model feels more open to me, and students respond more personally, I think making connections can elicit deeper, more thoughtful comprehension."

In both models—comprehension types and comprehension connections—students must use vocabulary from their reading to demonstrate comprehension. At the applied level and in all three connections areas, students use their own expressive vocabularies more often since these responses allow for more personal reactions than do the literal and interpretive level questions.

> **Extend Your Thinking**
>
> Unlike Terry, Jackie usually prefers to preteach the vocabulary words she believes are most important and necessary to help her students comprehend a selection. Which words in the bald eagle example do you think Jackie might preteach, and why?

Comprehension as Synthesis

Some teachers prefer to add *synthesis* as another aspect of comprehension. Keene and Zimmerman (2007) explain that synthesis occurs when we combine the conclusions we make as we read and then organize what we have learned into something greater than the sum of its parts. Synthesis means using ideas and information to create new understandings. A synthesis is not a summary that contains the main points of a piece. A synthesis of the bald eagle passage in Figure 2.1 might read something like this: "There are more eagles today than there were in the past. But we must be afraid they will disappear because the federal government still protects the 59 eagle species. Or are the laws no longer necessary?" This observation shows literal, interpretive, and applied comprehension, as well as connections to self, to the text, and, because the student gained information about other eagle species from other sources, connections to the world. Additionally, notice the question that ends this synthesis: "Or are the laws no longer necessary?" The reader who comprehends deeply often has questions that result from synthesizing the information he or she has read. This kind of thoughtful reading comprehension is what we want to develop in students.

How does vocabulary knowledge relate to synthesis? Is it enough to know the key words in this short passage? Sure, knowing the key words is necessary to comprehend the passage. To comprehend the few sentences in the synthesis above and the entire passage about eagles, a student needs to know the meaning of *migratory, endangered, abundant, symbol, opportunistic, old-growth,* and *captivity*. But notice the variety of words (e.g., *Northwest, hatchling, chemicals, pollution, environment, extinct*) a student might use in connecting to the text and synthesizing what he or she learned. Clearly, these words are not in the passage, but they may be in students' personal lexicon or dictionary. Making connections that include synthesizing allows students to tap their prior knowledge. They make new meanings and build rich concepts when they use the vocabulary they already possess and weave it into the vocabulary they see in print.

Reciprocal Comprehension

Reciprocal teaching (Oczkus, 2010), in which students take on roles, is another way to build comprehension. While each role requires recognizing and using vocabulary, one role focuses specifically on new and/or difficult vocabulary.

Teaching in Action

After modeling the roles with her students, Laurie, a fourth-grade teacher, puts students in groups of four and gives each student a different role:

- *Questioner: Ask questions you have about the text or that will help others understand the text better.*
- *Predictor: Make guesses or predictions about what you think might happen next in the text.*
- *Summarizer: Note important points and give a brief overview of the ideas in the text.*
- *Clarifier: Identify difficult vocabulary and make hard concepts clear for the group.*

Laurie finds reciprocal teaching an effective way to develop comprehension with both fiction and nonfiction material. She believes reciprocal teaching helps make content reading, with its heavy vocabulary load, more understandable. She says, "I arrange groups so each group has at least one 'high flier' and one student who struggles with reading. I often assign the 'high flier' as the Predictor or Summarizer and the struggling student as Clarifier or Questioner. This is a slight adaptation of the original method because I encourage my struggling students to identify vocabulary that is difficult for them and also ask questions they have about the selection. Both Clarifier and Questioner roles allow students who have trouble reading to contribute in important ways by stimulating the discussion with questions about difficult words and concepts. The 'high flier' students help struggling students by predicting and summarizing, both skills that require good comprehension of a selection."

The Next Step in Vocabulary Instruction © 2012 by Karen Bromley, Scholastic Teaching Resources

Students are encouraged to affix sticky notes to pages on which they write their questions, difficult or important vocabulary words, predictions, and points to remember when summarizing. When students discuss the selection, the Questioner and Clarifier lead the discussion with the Summarizer and Predictor interjecting their contributions when appropriate.

Laurie does not usually preteach vocabulary. She believes reciprocal teaching offers students an opportunity to use their own word-attack skills independently or to get help from each other. Like Laurie, you can encourage students to pose questions to one another such as "How did you figure that word out?" and "How did you know that?" so they can share their own personal word-attack and comprehension strategies. Often, students learn more from one another during small-group work in reciprocal teaching than what you can accomplish in a large-group setting.

We know that comprehension means "bringing meaning to print" as well as "taking meaning from print." The meaning students bring to print includes their own prior knowledge, or schema, the words and concepts they have stored in their heads, and the knowledge they have about the genre or format of what they are about to read. For example, knowing a little bit about eagles helps a student read and learn more about them from a chapter or book on eagles. But, if a student is going to read about eagles on a Web site like www.turtlebay.org/eaglecam, which contains a webcam of an eagle's nest, it's also important to know how to locate the Web site, where to click to find a picture of the nest, and how to access an explanation of the picture. The meaning students take from print or from viewing Internet information includes the new information as well as the mental images that arise from weaving their own knowledge with the new knowledge.

Clearly, there are different models for improving comprehension, but some form of vocabulary instruction occurs in all of them. Some of that direct vocabulary instruction is done by the teacher and some of it is done in guided practice situations. But remember that knowing the meanings of difficult words and concepts is at the heart of comprehension, no matter which model or combination of models you decide to follow.

Wide Reading Promotes Comprehension

Wide reading means reading and listening to books from all genres (fantasy, realistic fiction, folktales, poetry, biography, historical fiction, and nonfiction). Reading widely builds rich vocabulary vicariously, promotes comprehension, and broadens a student's understanding of different writing styles and formats. Deep reading means reading thoughtfully, while interpreting and analyzing what one reads. Wide and deep reading translate to word learning and comprehension, and also to good writing. Through wide and deep reading, students build visual memories for how words look; thus, they are able to spell and use words more effectively as writers.

To, With, and By Reading

Reading is often characterized as "to, with, and by." When students read widely and deeply, each kind of reading builds vocabulary and comprehension. In each type of reading, you invite students to use their prior knowledge and schema to make predictions, ask questions, and interpret, discuss, and otherwise be involved in making sense out of print. Whenever possible, in each type of reading, I believe students should have choices in the text they listen to. When students choose a subject of interest, they have a personal connection and a purpose for engaging with an author's words, and this improves their word learning and comprehension.

- **"To" reading** is oral reading done for students by a teacher, parent, caregiver, sibling, or on a recording. Listening to stories read aloud adds to a student's fund of words and concepts. During read-alouds, you build vocabulary and concepts as you read books of all types and engage students in appropriate discussions that clarify new words and encourage their opinions and predictions. Research shows that repeated readings of the same story combined with direct instruction in targeted words increase the vocabularies of young students (Beck & McKeown, 2007). Read-alouds give students the opportunity to acquire ideas from texts that are above their reading levels and that do not appear in books they routinely choose to read. For example, primary-grade teachers can introduce children to scientific terms through teacher-led read-alouds (Heisey & Kucan, 2010).

VOCABULARY BUILDING BOOKS

- *Big Words for Little People* by Jamie Lee Curtis (HarperCollins, 2008). (Grades K–3). This book uses rhyming prose and colorful characters to introduce young children to big words like *amazing, hilarious, spectacular, stunning, competent, rotund, reside, supreme,* and *intelligence.*

- *Donovan's Word Jar* by Monalisa DeGross (HarperTrophy, 1998). (Grades 3–6). A young African-American boy loves new words and collects them on slips of paper in his word jar. His grandmother helps him figure out what to do when the jar is full.

- *Miss Alaineus: A Vocabulary Disaster* by Debra Frasier (Harcourt, 2000). (Grades 2–6). Sage, a girl who is home with the flu, misunderstands the weekly vocabulary words her friend gives her over the telephone in this funny story filled with the alphabet and many words for each letter. Directions for having a "Vocabulary Parade," along with a sample letter home explaining it to parents, are included.

- *A Series of Unfortunate Events Box: The Complete Wreck* (Books 1–13) by Lemony Snicket (HarperCollins, 2006). (Grades 3–9). These stories about the unlucky adventures of three orphaned children are full of colorful and sophisticated words, with each word's definition woven into the story to help students understand word meanings.

- *Martin's Big Words: The Life of Dr. Martin Luther King, Jr.* by Doreen Rappaport (Hyperion, 2001). (Grades 3–8). This biography of Martin Luther King, Jr., tells his story through the big words that affected him and many other African Americans. Terms like "White Only," "Freedom," "Peace" and "You are as good as anyone" appear in bold and color print.

- *The Big Book of Words for Curious Kids* by Heloise Antoine (Peachtree, 1995). (Grades 1–3). Filled with drawings of a variety of objects and their printed names, this book engages young children and ELLs as they learn new words. (Antoine has written other "big books of words," including *Curious Kids Go to Preschool* and *Curious Kids Go On Vacation.*)

- *Is There Really a Human RACE?* by Jamie Lee Curtis (HarperCollins, 2006). (Grades 2–5). This story plays on the multiple meanings of the word *race* as Curtis asks all sorts of amusing questions about humanity.

Of course, all children's books provide opportunities to learn new vocabulary; however, some books specifically extend vocabulary in unique ways by using challenging, multisyllabic words and explaining them within the story in creative and relevant ways (see page 32). But talk that accompanies read-alouds is critical to helping students acquire vocabulary and concepts. Teacher-led discussions and questions prompt students to think more deeply and acquire words and sophisticated knowledge they might not otherwise acquire.

- **"With" reading** is reading that includes the student as a participant and is often called "shared reading" or "interactive reading." In the classroom, this kind of reading often involves having children supply vocabulary, finish sentences, point to pictures, take turns reading parts of the story, ask and answer questions, and otherwise be actively engaged in the reading with another person. Predictable books, like those written by Mary Ann Hoberman and illustrated by Michael Emberly (see below), are ideal for shared reading at home. In these stories, one sentence appears on the left side of the page in one color and the next sentence appears on the right side of the page in another color. The combination of sentence placement and color allows for easy shared reading between two people, while colorful pictures support the text.

BOOKS FOR SHARED READING

Written by Mary Ann Hoberman and Illustrated by Michael Emberly

- *You Read to Me, I'll Read to You: Very Short Fairy Tales to Read Together* (Little, Brown, 2004)
- *You Read to Me, I'll Read to You: Very Short Mother Goose Tales to Read Together* (Little, Brown, 2005)
- *You Read to Me, I'll Read to You: Very Short Stories to Read Together* (Little, Brown, 2001)
- *You Read to Me, I'll Read to You: Very Short Scary Tales to Read Together* (Little, Brown, 2009)

- **"By" reading** is reading done alone by the student. This kind of independent reading should occur with easy material that is written on the student's independent reading level. For easy independent reading, the student should recognize about 98 percent of the words encountered and comprehend about 95 percent of what is read. Students learn more about words and their meanings each time they reread stories themselves that they have previously heard read by others and/or read with others. So, send books home that you have read with students in school and encourage parents to read these same books with their children. Seeing and hearing words several times helps students learn and remember them.

  Graphic novels are an increasingly popular book genre and one that is embraced by students as independent reading material at all grade levels. Graphic novels contain pictures and fewer words than typical stories, so they are easier to read. They include cartoon-like drawings, words in speech bubbles, captions, and labels for objects, and students are drawn to them. Graphic novels appear today in every genre, even unexpected ones, such as biography, historical fiction, and nonfiction. So don't overlook making these books available to your students for their independent reading. Graphic novels can do a great deal to increase students' motivation to read as well as their vocabularies and comprehension.

GRAPHIC NOVELS

Graphic novels are actually comics in book format and include sequential art and print that is especially attractive to reluctant readers, struggling readers, and English learners. Color illustrations, conversation bubbles, unexpected formats, and fewer words than typical texts help promote easy comprehension. You can use graphic novels as a way to develop students' visual and media literacy and as a bridge to electronic literacy. Here are a few of the many kid-friendly fiction and nonfiction graphic novels suggested by the Junior Library Guild for students in grades 2–6 (www.juniorlibraryguild.com). At this Web site, you will also find lists, reviews, and titles of award-winning graphic novels for teens.

- *A Very Babymouse Christmas: Babymouse #15* by Jennifer Holm (Random House, 2011) (one of 15 books in the Babymouse series). Babymouse searches for her Christmas presents and daydreams about Babyrudolph and Babyscrooge, but wants to receive a special present.

- *Benjamin Bear in Fuzzy Thinking* by Philippe Coudray (Toon, 2010). Among other silly things, Benjamin Bear tries sharing his sweater without taking it off and using a rabbit to dry dishes. Ink, conversation bubbles, and full-color illustrations show how he solves these problems.

- *True Things (Adults Don't Want Kids to Know): Amelia Rules!* by Jimmy Gownley (Atheneum, 2010). Amelia's 11th year begins with a birthday party, but things quickly go downhill. Aunt Tanner would usually help—but she is hardly ever around. Full-color illustrations and text tell the story.

- *Amelia Earhart: This Broad Ocean* by Sarah Stewart Taylor, illustrations by Ben Towle (Hyperion, 2011). In this award-winning graphic novel, an aspiring young journalist named Grace is excited when Amelia Earhart arrives in Newfoundland on her way to becoming the first female passenger to cross the Atlantic Ocean by air. Grace watches as Amelia and her pilot take off and then gets Earhart's telegram announcing their arrival in Ireland 20 hours later.

Also check the America Library Association Web site (www.ala.org) and the University of Wisconsin-Madison's Cooperative Children's Book Center Web site (www.education.wisc.edu/ccbc/books/graphicnovels.asp;2008) for more information and other titles of graphic novels.

What Is Fluency?

Fluency, a foundational element of the Common Core State Standards, is not just about rate or speed of reading. It includes prosody, which is the expression, stress, phrasing, and rhythm of oral language, as well as comprehension, which is the meaning a reader makes of print while reading. Good readers exhibit fluency that includes prosody and comprehension. Students who are fluent readers are usually good comprehenders. They connect with print, know the words they meet, notice and use punctuation correctly, and read easily with appropriate expression, stress, and phrasing. Vocabulary knowledge is a huge contributor to fluency. In fact, by some estimates, vocabulary comprises as much as 70–80 percent of fluency (Fuchs, Fuchs, Hosp, & Jenkins, 2001). Fluent readers

Extend Your Thinking

How would you accommodate students who cannot fluently read the science or social studies texts you are expected to use at your grade level?

The Next Step in Vocabulary Instruction © 2012 by Karen Bromley, Scholastic Teaching Resources

recognize and understand many words, and they read more quickly and easily than those with smaller vocabularies.

"Just Right" Fluency

Fluency is a tricky thing. The right amount of fluency in oral or silent reading is important. Too little or too much fluency can be a problem. A lack of fluency in reading difficult material means reading at such a slow rate that readers can't remember what they just read. Thus, they have poor comprehension. Too much fluency or an abnormally fast reading rate may not support comprehension either. This happens when students read so quickly that they don't have time to process the words they meet. An unusually fast rate of oral or silent reading can translate to poor comprehension as well.

Think about reading two books: a chapter book, like *Because of Winn-Dixie* by Kate DiCamillo (Candlewick, 2000), and a chemistry textbook. *Because of Winn-Dixie* is written on about a fourth-grade level, and all the words DiCamillo uses are already in your own sight vocabulary. The chemistry text might be written on a 12th-grade level and, depending on your background, many of the words in the text are probably not in your sight word vocabulary. You will be able to comprehend and read *Because of Winn-Dixie* at a faster rate than you can comprehend and read the chemistry text. In order to understand the chemistry text, you will need to adjust your reading speed by reading more slowly to accommodate the vocabulary and concept load. And, if you tried to read the chemistry text at the same rate of speed as you read *Because of Winn-Dixie*, your comprehension would probably be miserable, to say the least. So, faster reading does not always result in better comprehension.

"Reading fluency has become a speed reading contest and divorced from the essence of reading—comprehension" (Rasinski & Hamman, 2010). In some schools, students who read slowly and haltingly go to the school's fluency lab, where they are timed as they practice reading passages orally. The goal is to improve their reading rate, but the mistaken notion is that once the rate improves, so will comprehension. Unfortunately, the message this conveys is a bad one. Students begin to believe that "reading fast means I am a good reader." The ultimate goal should be to read smoothly and quickly enough, with proper expression and inflections, so that comprehension occurs easily.

An analogy to comprehension and rate of reading is driving a car within posted speed limits. In most countries, speed limits are usually posted on roads and highways. These signs let drivers know the appropriate speed for the type of road, geography, and population density of the area through which the road passes. Speed limits let a driver know how fast to sensibly drive without risking an accident. Rate of reading is not quite as easy for readers, because no speed limit signs are posted. Background knowledge and word knowledge should help a sensitive reader (whose goal is comprehension) to read at a rate that is comfortable and affords understanding of text, but good readers must also be aware of their own speed limits so they do not sacrifice comprehension for speed.

Extend Your Thinking

What do you think the goals of a fluency program should be? What would you include in a fluency lab like the one described above in order for such a program to be effective?

Try using the speed limit analogy with your students to help them modulate their rate if they read too quickly and have comprehension problems. For students who read slowly and haltingly, try having them read material they are interested in that has fewer difficult words and concepts to master. This should improve their fluency and give them confidence to tackle more difficult text. So, help your students develop their reading rate by encouraging them to read widely and deeply about topics that interest them and in materials that are easy to read.

What Makes Words Stick?

In order for students to comprehend and read fluently, they need to possess large vocabularies. How do you learn best? Have you recently learned or tried to learn something new—a sport or hobby, for example? As a beginning golfer, to make the game really "stick" in my head, I took lessons from a local teaching pro who demonstrated how to hold and swing a club. She used golf vocabulary such as *shaft, head, grip, hosel,* and *chip* with me. I immersed myself in the sport by using these terms as I talked with friends who were golfers and asked questions about local courses and advice on the best golf equipment to purchase. I joined a weekly nine-hole golf league. I watched the Golf Channel to see how the experts play the game. I even practiced swinging the clubs and hitting balls by myself in the backyard.

To become a golfer, I learned from *demonstration* and *immersion* in the sport. According to Cambourne (1988), we learn literacy in the same way, through these two essential components. So, to become good comprehenders and fluent readers, students need to see many demonstrations of how words are used, how to use context and word parts to figure out unknown words, and how to use word-attack strategies to infer meaning. As with my self-immersion in golf, students need to be deeply involved in learning and using vocabulary as they read and write.

If you work with English language learners, there are some specific ways to help them learn new words that work for struggling English speakers, too. Both groups can benefit from your usual direct instruction and guided practice as they learn new words. But teaching unfamiliar words is even more effective, for ELLs especially (Manyak & Bauer, 2009), when you do the following:

- Talk slowly and enunciate clearly
- Simplify the grammar you use
- Repeat explanations
- Supply synonyms
- Use concrete objects, images, graphic organizers, and drama

Teach Words Directly

Through teacher modeling and think-alouds, you can provide direct instruction to *demonstrate* the use of context, word parts, and other word-attack strategies to help your students infer meanings of new words. Read-alouds are an excellent way to do this and to demonstrate fluency and comprehension strategies. After reading, you can immerse students in guided practice and independent activities in which they apply the strategy you have modeled to new words, or use the target vocabulary in other activities.

 The Next Step in Vocabulary Instruction © 2012 by Karen Bromley, Scholastic Teaching Resources

Teaching in Action

After reading The Great Kapok Tree *by Lynne Cherry (Harcourt Brace, 1990), Annette told her students that when she first read the book, she didn't recognize the word* destruction. *She used a think-aloud to model how she decoded the word:*

"I thought about construct, *a word I know that means 'to make,' and then I thought about 'de' in* desist, *which means 'to stop.' That helped me guess that* destruction *means 'to stop making something.' When I read the story, I realized that* destruction *means even more. It means 'to ruin.'"*

In this way, Annette modeled for students how she used word parts and context to decode a difficult word.

ACTIVITY ■ Word of the Week

Materials: chart paper and marker or white board, sticky notes

Word of the Week is another example of direct instruction that extends students' multisyllabic vocabularies. Write a word like *bloviation* on chart paper or the white board on Monday (see Figure 2.2).

Teach the word by giving its use in a sentence first; for example, "I was talking to an old friend who said she hoped there wouldn't be a lot of *bloviation* from the speakers at our next high school reunion." Ask students what the word might mean and then give its dictionary meaning ("to speak or write verbosely or windily"). Last, focus on

Word of the Day
?????
bloviation

Figure 2.2 *Feature a "Word of the Week" to grow students' vocabularies.*

word parts to connect its meaning to something known (*blo-* may be derived from the word *blow*) and syllables (blo-vi-a-tion) to aid in pronunciation. Then challenge students to use the word appropriately the rest of the week in conversations and/or writing. When students use the word correctly, have them note it on sticky notes and affix them to the chart or whiteboard. On Friday, review and honor the many different ways students used the word. After you have chosen the word of the week a few times, students enjoy choosing and presenting the weekly word themselves.

Provide Guided Practice

After you have taught words directly and modeled several think-alouds, you can provide guided practice to immerse students in word learning together. Once you have modeled how you unlock new words, have students think aloud to show each other the strategies they use. Students enjoy and learn a lot from each other when they work in pairs to practice and share their word-attack strategies. Here are other guided practice activities that immerse students in learning and remembering words.

ACTIVITY ■ Readers Theater

Readers Theater is a dramatic presentation of a written work in script form. Students read from a script, and parts are divided among the readers. No memorization, costumes, props, or special lighting is needed. Since the focus is on reading the text with expressive voices, the material should be easy enough so that students don't stumble over too many difficult words, although it can include a few new words.

Teaching in Action

Annette, a third-grade teacher, uses Readers Theater to immerse her students in word learning, fluency, and comprehension. On the Internet, she found a Web page for Readers Theater plays and scripts (www.teachingheart. net/readerstheater.htm), and she printed the script for The Great Kapok Tree. This Web page includes free, printable scripts based on many children's books, tips for using Readers Theater, ways to take a favorite story and turn it into an outstanding script, and ideas for evaluating the activity.

Annette chose this particular script because she had already read the story to her students, and it had 14 parts that would accommodate her entire class (with some students reading parts in pairs and everyone reading in chorus). She also found videos of different classes performing The Great Kapok Tree on YouTube and showed these demonstrations to her students as an introduction (www.youtube.com/watch?v=1WUL_pSXQcA). Then Annette immersed students in the activity by assigning parts and having them practice by reading and rereading their parts (and those read by the chorus) in pairs. Students helped each other with difficult vocabulary, and Annette circulated among students to provide help.

Annette's class performed several times before they invited other K–3 classes into the library to see their production. They decorated the library to look like a jungle with green crepe paper streamers, pictures of the animals labeled with their names, and green plants borrowed from classrooms. Annette said, "This production was so valuable in motivating my students for doing more Readers Theater, and other teachers wanted the name of the Web site so they could do Readers Theater with their students. I think it helps make students aware of how they can read with a dramatic voice, and so it makes for better word recognition, comprehension, and fluency."

> ### Extend Your Thinking
>
> Read *The Fluent Reader* (Rasinski, 2010). It is packed with oral reading strategies for building word recognition, fluency, and comprehension. Rasinski includes strategies like read-alouds, supported reading, repeated reading, Readers Theater, and more.

Have students work with a buddy, partners, or individually during and after wide and deep reading as they engage in other guided practice activities to stretch their vocabularies.

ACTIVITY ■ Word Jar

Materials: a large plastic jar or fish bowl with a wide mouth, 5-inch by 8-inch index cards, tape or glue, markers, *Donovan's Word Jar* by Monalisa DeGross (HarperTrophy, 1998) or *Max's Words* by Kate Banks (Farrar, Straus & Giroux, 2006)

This activity involves having students collect random words in a large container.

1. First read and talk about these books with your students:
    *   *Donovan's Word Jar*: In this story, a young African-American boy loves new words and collects them on slips of paper in a jar. His grandmother helps him figure out what to do when the jar is full.

The Next Step in Vocabulary Instruction © 2012 by Karen Bromley, Scholastic Teaching Resources

- *Max's Words*: When Max's older brothers collect stamps and coins, he decides to collect words. When one word leads to another and he has a story, Max must also find pictures.

2. Display a jar or fish bowl labeled "Word Jar" (see Figure 2.3).

3. Have students add an important, new, or interesting word to the Word Jar as they hear words during read-alouds or as they read on their own. Students print the word, the title and author of the story from which it comes, and his or her name on one side of an index card. On the reverse side, they write a sentence that contains the word.

4. Students can pull individual cards from the Word Jar and learn words on their own or with a partner. Or, they can remove 10–12 word cards randomly, arrange the words in some type of order, and tell a story about them as Max does in *Max's Words*.

Writing a word in the context of a sentence gives students an opportunity to practice using the word appropriately. Providing the title and author of the story gives classmates ideas for books they might want to read later. Putting new words together in a jar makes a repository of important, new, and interesting words that students can review with a partner during free time. It is a novel way to increase and broaden vocabularies. You might even limit the words added to the Word Jar to multisyllabic words and challenge students to learn and recite ten new words a week from the jar for a partner.

Figure 2.3 *A classroom Word Jar holds many possibilities for building vocabulary.*

ACTIVITY ■ Word Walls

Materials: file folders, scissors, markers

Another example of guided practice that immerses students in words is the use of Word Walls. Most K–3 teachers routinely list words on bulletin boards to help students recognize, say, spell, and use them in their writing (see Figure 2.4 on the next page). They use games like "I'm Thinking of . . ." to encourage students to identify and pronounce words on the Word Wall. For example, the teacher (or a student) gives a clue like, "I'm thinking of a word that means *great*." Students then search the Word Wall for the word, and one student is called on who might answer, "Are you thinking of *terrific*?" This kind of immersion and engagement with words is a fun way to build students' vocabulary reservoirs.

Upper-grade teachers find that Word Walls improve their students' writing. They create a Word Wall to accompany a science or social studies unit or a wall of "Random $1,000 Words" that holds interesting, descriptive words such as *enormous, undignified*, and *flagrant*. Another kind of Word Wall is a portable one made from file folders (see Figure 2.5 on the next page). Students can make their own by measuring 26 squares and labeling each with a letter of the alphabet. Then, as students meet new words, they can write them in the appropriate box. These Word Walls serve as a resource for students who can review their own personally chosen words and then use them in their writing.

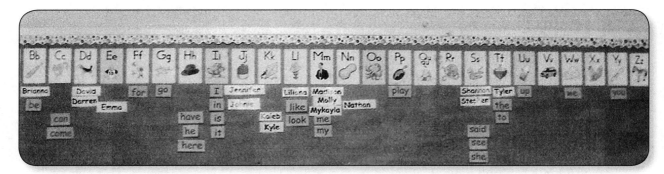

Figure 2.4 *Students use Word Walls as resources when they write.*

Try Independent Activities

You have just read about direct instruction that involves demonstration, and guided practice that involves immersion in experiences to build vocabulary. Direct instruction occurs when you introduce and explicitly teach new words to students before, during, and after reading. Guided practice offers students opportunities to use words that typically have been introduced to them. There are many ways to immerse

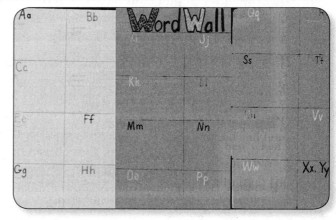

Figure 2.5 *A fifth-grade student made his own personal, portable Word Wall.*

students independently, both in and out of school, to broaden and enrich their vocabularies and aid their comprehension and fluency. Since students usually spend more hours per week outside school than in school, it is a good idea to capitalize on their out-of-school time. The following independent activities can strengthen the home-school connection, too. The activities require small amounts of time and can be adapted according to students' abilities. Note that these collector activities are adapted from Smith (2008).

ACTIVITY ■ World Collector

Materials: a small notebook for each student*, pens or markers

- Have students collect new or interesting words (on their way to school, in a restaurant, watching television, listening to music, at the playground, gym, library, mall, and so on).

- Tell students to listen, observe, think, and list new or interesting words in a World Collector Field Book.

- Ask students to share their lists with one another once a week.

* You can buy these small notebooks cheaply at a discount store.

The Next Step in Vocabulary Instruction © 2012 by Karen Bromley, Scholastic Teaching Resources

ACTIVITY ■ Category Collector

Materials: World Collector Field Book from previous activity, pens or markers

- As homework, give each student a different category (e.g., round things, flat things, tiny things, things from trees, things that possess computers, tools, purple things, and so on).
- Have students make a list of different things that fit the category in their World Collector Field Book and then share their lists the next day with a partner.

ACTIVITY ■ Object Collector

Materials: a gallon-size plastic bag and 20 sticky notes for each student, markers or pens

- Challenge students to collect 20 objects they find over a weekend, name each object by attaching a sticky note to it, and place it in the bag.
- Have students bring the bag to school on Monday and tell a story about each named object and its relation to themselves.

ACTIVITY ■ Curiosity Collector

Materials: a quart-size plastic bag and 10 sticky notes for each student, markers or pens

- Challenge students to collect 10 very small things they don't understand or things that have a special meaning for them (e.g., clothespin, bobby pin, staple, eraser, grocery list, letter, and so on) and place them in the bag.
- Have students label each object with a sticky note and share them with a partner at school, explaining how the object connects to them personally.

Experiences like these with a range of words that immerse students in learning words on their own, along with wide independent reading, help broaden and enrich their vocabularies, comprehension, and fluency. You can reinforce these experiences and the words students collect by making master lists of these "found" words on a transparency and share them on a document camera or a SMART Board. Or, you can devote a Word Wall bulletin board to these collected words. The Word Wall gives students access to the words for writing and other activities.

Daily Calendar: Round-the-Clock Vocabulary

Vocabulary building is especially important for students who have not had the benefit of the background experiences, prior knowledge, reading models, and oral language interactions that build vocabulary naturally. Because students take in new knowledge most easily when they connect it to what they already know, background information and concepts play a key role in learning new words and reading comprehension. Direct and intentional instruction build concepts students may have missed or only partially learned. Of course, teaching vocabulary when you teach reading is a given, but vocabulary instruction must also occur when you teach science, social studies, math, health, and language arts.

Are you carefully selecting key vocabulary and preteaching word meanings and pronunciation before or after your students read a story or other text in science or social studies? That's great—keep it up! But don't stop there—vocabulary instruction should not be left to 10 minutes a day before or after a lesson. Your vocabulary instruction should be comprehensive—it should happen throughout the entire day whenever opportunities arise. Teaching new words all day long is important because word knowledge aids comprehension, oral reading fluency, writing, and learning in every subject. Once you begin to think about making vocabulary a round-the-clock enterprise, you'll find many ways to fit it into the big and little time slots from 8 a.m. to 3:20 p.m. The Daily Calendar: Round-the-Clock Vocabulary is packed with teacher-tested ideas that build vocabulary through demonstration, immersion, and engagement. You can send these ideas home for parents, siblings, and caregivers to use, or you can select activities to do in the classroom with individuals, small groups, or the entire class.

DAILY CALENDAR: ROUND-THE-CLOCK VOCABULARY

8 a.m. Introduce a Mystery Word of the Day. Start each day with a new word (a seasonal word or one related to a content-area unit). Write it in a sentence on the board. Include context so students can infer the word's meaning (i.e., "The fall apple harvest brings lots of pickers to the orchard.") When students first come into the classroom in the morning, have them read the sentence and talk with a buddy about the word's meaning or look it up in a dictionary. Then have them write the sentence, word, and its definition in a Vocabulary Notebook. (A spiral-bound notebook makes a great journal. Have students label two or three pages for each letter of the alphabet, number the pages, and make a table of contents for easy use.)

8:10 a.m. Reinforce Menu Words. On Monday morning, put the week's lunch menu on a transparency and, when you take lunch count each day, have a student use a pointer to lead the class in chorally reading the lunch words. You'll be surprised at how many new words students pick up with this little add-on to your regular vocabulary teaching!

8:15 a.m. Preteach Reading Vocabulary. As you introduce a story for silent reading, teach three to five words you think students do not know but absolutely need to know to understand the story. Write the words in sentences on the board, an overhead transparency, or chart paper. Define the words and, to build on students' background knowledge, have them supply related words, synonyms, or antonyms. This connects what students already know to the new words and helps ensure their learning. Use a colored marker to underline roots and affixes. List other words students know that look like, sound like, or have similar meanings to the new words. Have students use the new words in sentences. You've addressed several multiple intelligences with this strategy.

8:55 a.m. Do Postreading Review. Write a list of recently introduced words from a story on the board or chart paper (e.g., *distraught, failure, frown, difficult*). Have students play the game "I'm Thinking of . . ." Begin with a sentence such as, "I'm thinking of a word that means the same as *upset* or *troubled*." Call on a student, who might say, "Are you thinking of *distraught*?" and answer, "Yes, I am thinking of *distraught*" as you check off or erase the word. "I'm Thinking of . . ." gives students meaningful repetition and practice, and they must speak in complete sentences!

 The Next Step in Vocabulary Instruction © 2012 by Karen Bromley, Scholastic Teaching Resources

9:00 a.m. Teach Problem-Solving Words in Math. Scan the word problems your students will read this morning and select a key term from each (e.g., *greater than, estimate, shorter, equal to*). As you read each problem together, before students solve them, preteach these problem-solving words. Give examples and draw a picture on the board to show what each term means. (For *greater than*, draw one glass of water more full than another; for *estimate*, draw a stick-person with a cartoon bubble that reads, "My guess is . . ."). Remember: a picture is worth a thousand words!

9:40 a.m. Line Up With Adjectives. When it's time to line up for music (or gym or art), have students take their place in line by saying an adjective that begins with the same letter as their name (e.g., Wallace— wicked, Susan—sincere, Raymond—rhythmic). This is a great way to build descriptive language!

9:45 a.m. Collaborate in Music. Plan ahead with your school's music teacher to sing songs with students that correlate with your science or social studies unit. This activity uses song lyrics to expose students to words and concepts associated with the content you are teaching and reinforces these words in a meaningful context.

10:15 a.m. Provide Tools for Writing Workshop. Encourage students to use interesting and descriptive words and give them the resources to do it! On the computer(s) in your classroom, bookmark a student dictionary like those described and linked at www.surfnetkids.com/dictionary.htm and equip your classroom with several age-appropriate thesauruses and dictionaries. During Author Share time, as students read their writing to the class, praise unusual or powerful word use. Add these to your Word Wall and have students add a word or two a day to their Vocabulary Notebooks. This is a great way to recognize each student's word use and stretch everyone's vocabulary!

11:15 a.m. Line Up With ABCs. As students begin to line up for lunch, have one student say a word that begins with an *A*, another student say a word that begins with a *B*, and so on, until everyone is in line. Encourage the use of unusual and new words recently learned. This develops fluency and creativity as students think on their feet.

11:25 a.m. Lunch and Learn. Eat lunch with ELLs and have them teach you, in their first language, the names of the foods you are eating. Then teach them the equivalent English words. (Do the same for color words, number words, and names of things in the cafeteria.) Taking time for one-on-one conversations like this helps you get to know students, builds their confidence, and develops both your vocabularies!

12:30 p.m. Think Aloud As You Read Aloud. When you come to a difficult word in a read-aloud, show students how you figure out its meaning from context.

- *For example: "I know that* descend *means 'to come down from a higher place,' because there are some clues in the sentence that tell me this. 'The monkey descended from the top of the tree.' 'From the top' gives me a picture of the monkey coming down the tree."*

Show students how you associate a new word with words you already know to figure out meaning.

- *For example: "That word* pacifist *reminds me of* Pacific *and* pacifier, *and they are related to* peaceful, *so a* pacifist *is probably someone who believes in peace."*

Thinking aloud gives students a window into your thinking as you model word-solving strategies!

12:50 p.m. Transition With "Earthquake." Choose a word like *planets* that contains several consonants and at least two vowels and have students "shake it up" to form new words. At first, pair students to provide a supportive model for struggling students. Have pairs put each letter of the word on a separate index card and then rearrange cards to make smaller words. Tell students to take turns manipulating letters to form words and writing them on a list. Compare lists to see which pair made the most words and caused the biggest "Earthquake"!

1:00 p.m. Use "Web-a-Word" in Social Studies. To introduce a new word like *telephoto* and teach the meanings of Greek and Latin roots, e.g., *tele* (far), *duct* (lead), *spect* (watch), first write the prefix, suffix, or root you intend to teach (and its meaning) on the board or chart paper. Then have students supply words that contain the target affix or root and write them on the web you've drawn below the word. Show students how to figure out the meanings of these words by using the meaning of the affix or root, e.g., *teleconference* means "to talk or confer from afar." The technical vocabulary of science and social studies is often based on Greek and Latin roots that require intentional teaching!

1:50 p.m. Transition With "$100 Words." Add to your class list of "$100 Words" by choosing a new word daily from the dictionary that students can use in their writing. Start the list on chart paper with the letter *A* and add a word a day until you have a word for the entire alphabet. Revisit the list daily when you have a spare minute or two, asking students to recall word meanings and pronunciations.

2:00 p.m. Review in Science. Divide your class into groups (four or five students each). Give each group a set of 3-inch by 5-inch tag board cards with the same 12–15 key words printed on them from the current unit. Have groups arrange words in a web or other graphic structure to show the relationships among them (e.g., *erupt, ash, dormant, lava, ooze, magma, mantle, crust, inner core, outer core, fault line, tectonic plate*). Encourage students to organize words in ways that make sense and then explain their thinking to the class. You can have students write each word's meaning on the back of its card. This strategy builds meaning vocabulary and helps give kids the "big picture" of the content you are studying.

2:40 p.m. Play Word Tag Before Art or PE. As students put away projects and books and clean up the room for the day before going to art or physical education, play Word Tag. Begin by identifying a category of words, such as nutrition. Then say a word like *yogurt* and ask a student to tag onto your word by saying a word that begins with the last letter of your word, e.g., *tomato*. The next student might say "onion," and so on.

3:20 p.m. Dismissal. Have students turn to a neighbor to share one new word they learned that day and use it in a sentence. Ask one or two students to use the Mystery Word of the Day in a sentence.

Congratulations! You've made vocabulary a round-the-clock teaching enterprise in your classroom and stretched your students' vocabularies immeasurably!

CHAPTER 3

Teaching Words Well

"I read a news article on Ken Green, a professional golfer who talked about an auto accident in which he lost his brother, girlfriend, dog, and had his right leg amputated. He said he was 'discombobulated' for quite awhile, but a prosthetic leg allowed him to golf again. The word 'discombobulated' isn't one I expected to read. When I told Ken's story to my seventh graders, I used the word because it seemed to describe perfectly how Ken must have felt."

—Mark, a seventh-
grade teacher

Word Consciousness

Mark appreciates the use of thought-provoking and vivid words. This quote is an example of how he displays an attitude of excitement and interest in words and language. This attitude is called "word consciousness" (Graves & Watts-Taffee, 2002). Teachers who are curious and passionate about words share their enthusiasm with students, and it becomes contagious. These teachers are excited about words and language. They appreciate out-of-the-ordinary, powerful, and appealing word use.

The Common Core State Standards (2011) require students to "demonstrate understanding of figurative language, relationships and nuances in word meanings." Mark knows this, so he shares new words like *discombobulated* with his students, and they talk about what the word communicates and other words that might do a better job or be less effective.

A second example of Mark's word consciousness often occurs during a typical teaching day, when his students encounter words with multiple meanings. Mark notes these words with the class and clarifies what they mean by asking students to offer their own paraphrased meanings. About 70 percent of the most frequently appearing words have multiple meanings (Lederer, 1991). For example, Mark might discuss a word like *spam* with its two meanings: 1) (capitalized) a canned meat and 2) junk mail on the Internet. They might discuss the three meanings of *java*: 1) (capitalized) an island in Indonesia, 2) a computer program, and 3) an informal term for coffee. Mark then might have his students brainstorm the different meanings for *hand*. There are at least five meanings: 1) to give someone something, 2) applause, 3) a way of measuring a horse's height, 4) cards dealt to someone playing a card game, and 5) the part of your arm at the end of your wrist. Mark says that both his students who are learning English and struggling readers need extra support with multiple-meaning words because these words can so easily disrupt comprehension.

A third example of Mark's word consciousness occurs when he shares words that have been recently added to *Merriam-Webster's Collegiate Dictionary*. He does this because he finds it fascinating himself, and it helps his students see that English grows and changes through slang, new technology, and the addition of foreign words. Did you know that new words become part of the dictionary every year after they have appeared in the media and public conversations over and over? (See Figure 3.1 for examples of these words). Mark reports that his students like being "in on" these new words and use them often after he shares them.

NEW WORDS RECENTLY ADDED TO THE DICTIONARY

automagically: automatically in a way that seems magical

bromance: close platonic male friendship

cheese ball: lacking taste or style

chillax: to calm down and relax

dead presidents: money in the form of bills

dog's breakfast: a confused mess

earjacking: eavesdropping on a conversation being carried on via a cellphone

gimme cap: a cap with a visor that often features a corporate logo or slogan

ginormous: a combination of gigantic and enormous

headbanger: a musician who performs hard rock; also: a fan of hard rock

killer app: a computer application that assures the success of the technology with which it is associated

LBD: little black dress

longneck: beer served in a bottle that has a long neck

lurk: to read messages on an Internet chat room

mouse potato: the online, wired generation's equivalent to couch potato

navel-gazing: useless or excessive self-contemplation

NIMBY: opposing the locating of something undesirable (not in my backyard)

sheepie: unquestioning follower

shopaholic: a person who is excessively fond of shopping

soft skills: characteristics that allow someone to interact with others harmoniously

staycation: vacation spent at home

swipeout: when the magnetic strip on a credit card wears out due to overuse

tankini: a woman's two-piece swimsuit consisting of bikini briefs and a tank top

tramp stamp: a tattoo

unfriend: to remove from a list of personal associates on a Web site

Sources: *Oxford Dictionary of English, New Oxford American Dictionary; Oxford English Dictionary; Merriam-Webster's Collegiate Dictionary. New Words* (2009)

Figure 3.1 *Share these new words with students to show your excitement about changes in the English language.*

The Next Step in Vocabulary Instruction © 2012 by Karen Bromley, Scholastic Teaching Resources

When you share unique words and word meanings, you heighten your students' awareness of the variety of words in the English language and the range of meanings they convey. In fact, as Lane and Allen report, "Promoting incidental learning and word consciousness through frequent and deliberate modeling of sophisticated vocabulary can add substantial breadth to students' vocabularies" (2010; p. 362).

Do you possess word consciousness? What do you know about word learning? How do you typically teach new words? How would you answer questions like these and the other questions shown in Figure 3.2? This kind of self-assessment and the reflection that should accompany it are the bread and butter of exemplary vocabulary instruction. What you believe, and what you know, dramatically affect how you teach.

VOCABULARY SELF-ASSESSMENT

- What do I know about word learning?
- What do I believe about the relationship among vocabulary, comprehension, and fluency?
- Do I possess word consciousness? Am I passionate and enthusiastic about word learning?
- Do I have a "can do" rather than a "can't do" attitude about students' word-learning abilities?
- How can I provide a vocabulary-rich environment and immerse students in new, important, and interesting words?
- How do I model word-learning strategies across the curriculum?
- How do I develop each student's independent word-learning strategies?
- Do I check to see if students already know the new words to be taught?
- Which words are central to the selection? Which words may reappear during the year?
- How do I vary the way I introduce new words? Who does the talking?
- How do I link students' prior knowledge to new words to make learning meaningful?
- How do I help students understand how to use context?
- How do I involve students in examining, manipulating, and processing new words?
- What activities do we do that include more than repetition? (e.g., practicing with context, examining word parts, investigating meaning, interacting with others)
- Do I assume that once I have taught a new word it has been learned?

Figure 3.2

Aspects of Word Learning

What do you believe and what do you assume about word learning? The four aspects discussed below are important to consider as you reflect on your answers to the self-assessment in Figure 3.2. Both theory and research evidence support these four aspects of word learning that are basic to the ideas in this book.

- *Personal*: Word learning is different for each learner because learners vary in what they know and how they learn words. Consequently, it is critical to tap prior knowledge and connect the *new* to what a student already *knows* (Fisher & Frey, 2008).

- *Active*: Word learning requires actively manipulating information and constructing meaning by thinking, talking, reading, writing, viewing, and doing in order to "own" new words. Students need multiple and varied opportunities to process words alone and in interactions with others (Stahl & Fairbanks, 1986).

- *Flexible*: Aspects of a word are not learned in a particular order; rather, learning is recursive. Students may learn a word's meaning before they learn to pronounce it and vice versa. Word learning may occur easily, without effort, or it may require intense, direct instruction using a variety of avenues (Gardner, 2000).

- *Strategic:* Word learning occurs when learners use different tools including context, structural analysis, meaning, associations, verbal processing, and so on. Students need to develop their own independent strategies for learning new words (Harmon, 2002).

Extend Your Thinking

How do you learn and remember a new word like *loquacious* (which means "talkative")? What other tips do you have for students who are trying to learn and remember new words?

Making vocabulary teaching direct, offering opportunities for guided practice, and doing independent work every day are important for ELLs and those who struggle with reading. Both groups need instruction not only in basic English vocabulary but also in the more sophisticated vocabulary of the content areas.

Direct "Deep" Teaching

To demonstrate one way to teach a word directly and "deeply" to students, I'll use the word *hosel* as an example. Let's assume that you don't know the word, that the word is necessary to understand a selection you are about to read, and that it is an important word for future reading. So, while I might not teach a word from a read-aloud in such depth since it might not be critical to comprehending today's text or important for future reading, I will spend time teaching *hosel* well.

To engage your prior knowledge, I might ask if you know the word, if you have ever heard or seen it, or if you know any words it reminds you of. This is a way to assess what, if any, knowledge students have of a new word, and it allows them to make a connection between what they know and what is new.

- If you answer "no" to these questions, I might say, "Do you see a word within *hosel* that you already know?" If you reply, "It looks like the word *hose* to me," I could say, "That's a good observation. The word *hosel* actually comes from a Dutch word similar to *hose*. *Hosel* means "to encase, bind, or restrict," just like panty hose encases or binds a person's legs and a garden hose restricts the flow of water to a stream." In this way, you connect *hosel* to hosiery or a garden hose so it helps you understand and remember it.

- If you answer "yes" to any of these questions, for example, you might say that you heard the word *hosel* while watching the Golf Channel, I might reply, "You're right, *hosel* has something to do with golf. Who knows the name of a well-known golfer?" If you answer "Phil Mickelson," I might say, "Phil usually never hits a ball on the *hosel*. Does that give you any clues to what the *hosel* is?"

After connecting what you know to new knowledge about *hosel*, I might ask questions to encourage you to guess where it might be located on a golf club. I could show you a picture of a golf club, and explain that this is the *hosel* (see Figure 3.3). I might ask what happens when Phil hits a ball on the *hosel*. I might ask you to use *hosel* orally in a sentence. I could also have you draw a picture to remind you of what *hosel* means and write a sentence in your vocabulary journal using the new word.

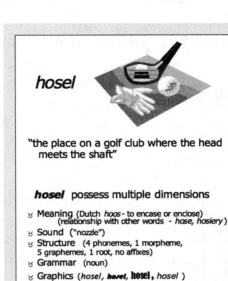

hosel

"the place on a golf club where the head meets the shaft"

hosel possess multiple dimensions

- ⋈ Meaning (Dutch *hoos* - to encase or enclose)
  (relationship with other words - *hose, hosiery*)
- ⋈ Sound ("nozzle")
- ⋈ Structure (4 phonemes, 1 morpheme, 5 graphemes, 1 root, no affixes)
- ⋈ Grammar (noun)
- ⋈ Graphics (*hosel, hosel,* **hosel**, *hosel*)

Extend Your Thinking

How does this example of vocabulary instruction demonstrate the characteristics of effective word learning? How was it personal, active, flexible, and strategic? How might you modify it to make it more effective?

Figure 3.3 *A picture is worth a thousand words when you teach a new word such as* hosel.

Knowing a Word Well

Word knowledge occurs on a continuum (Blachowicz & Fisher, 2002). Knowing a word begins with an introduction to the word, much like being introduced to someone when you initially learn his or her name. After spending time with that person, you may get to know him or her very well and you may become friends. Struggling students respond to an unknown word in much the same way. But, as students have opportunities to learn more about the unknown word and begin to recognize and use it, the word becomes familiar and they come to know the word well. When struggling students meet a new and difficult word, they may say one of several things: *I don't know the word. I have seen or heard it. I know something about it. I know it well.*

For students to know a word well, they must understand and know each dimension of it so they can use it appropriately. Just recognizing a word when reading is not enough to know it well. Just using a word when speaking is not enough. Students need to know what the word means and how to use it, say it, and spell it to know it well. To determine your students' knowledge of the new words in a science passage, for example, use this adaptation of the "Knowledge Rating Scale" (Blachowicz & Fisher, 2002) in the activity below.

ACTIVITY ▮ "Friend or Stranger?"

Ask students to rate their knowledge of several new words to determine which words to teach (see Figure 3.4). Responses on the scale suggest that you might want to review *glacier* quickly with this student, but you probably do not need to teach the word in depth. You will need to spend time teaching *esker* and *cirque* to this student, who seems to have little knowledge of either word. Since the student has some knowledge of *fiord,* you can tap his prior knowledge to determine what else you can do to help him know the word well.

"FRIEND OR STRANGER?" KNOWLEDGE RATING SCALE

How much do I know about these words?

	It's a stranger! (I don't know it.)	Have seen or heard it	Know something about it	Know what it means	Can say it correctly	Can spell and write it	It's a friend! "I know it well."
moraine			X				
esker	X						
fiord		X					
drumlin			X				
cirque	X						
glacier							X

Figure 3.4 *Use this scale to assess a student's knowledge of words.*

Guidelines for Instruction

There are many ways to provide direct instruction, guided practice, and independent activities to reinforce the meaning, pronunciation, and spelling of a new word like *hosel*. Along with what you have learned in chapters 1 and 2, and what you know about your own beliefs from answering the questions in the Vocabulary Self-Assessment, your knowledge of what constitutes good vocabulary teaching is important. Here are eight guidelines to keep in mind as you become more adept at teaching words well.

1. Select words and assess word knowledge. Look at the new words the basal or text suggests you should teach. Decide on each word's importance and long-term utility before teaching it. In some cases, students may already know a word, so you may not need to teach it. Consider the word's long-term usefulness. If it is a word that students do not know and if it may not appear again in any future reading, it is probably not worth teaching. If context will help students figure the word out on their own, don't bother to teach it either.

To tell if students already know a word, ask questions like those I asked you about the word *hosel* or use the "Friend or Stranger?" Knowledge Rating Scale activity. Or, for a simpler activity, have students assess their own word knowledge. Give them a list of the words they need to know to comprehend the passage or unit and that will be useful in future reading. Have students write one of these symbols beside each word:

+ know it	√ might know it	− don't know it

Then look at students' responses and determine which words to teach and who needs to know them before reading. This assessment lets you differentiate instruction, too. You may decide that some students can read independently without further vocabulary work and that others need some need direct instruction from you. Remember, though, that science, social studies, and math contain many conceptually dense terms, and most students need instruction in this technical vocabulary.

2. **Teach a few words directly and deeply.** Rather than teaching several words less well, teach a few important words deeply, especially Tier 2 and Tier 3 words. Explore word parts, meanings, usage, and the spelling and pronunciation of these words. In this regard, examine the list of do's and don'ts provided in Figure 3.5. While you may be tempted to introduce the entire list of new words that the basal or content text suggests, it is more effective to do the following:

- Limit the number of new words you teach so you do not put students into "cognitive overload."

- Teach no more than 3–5 new words at a time to students in grades 1–3 and no more than 4–6 new words to grades 4–8 students at a time.

- For struggling students and English language learners, teach fewer words.

- To make the new words stick, remember to connect words that students already know and that are related to the new words.

WHICH WORDS TO TEACH: SOME DO'S AND DON'T'S

Do's

- *Do select key words* that are essential or central to understanding the main concept(s) in the unit or lesson. (If students don't know these words, they probably won't understand the rest of the unit.)

- *Do look for words in italicized or boldface print.* Those words are often essential. (Highlighting focuses attention and usually denotes importance.)

- *Do select words that are repeated.* Repetition usually means that a word is important, and it can deepen students' understanding.

- *Do teach words that will be used in the future.* Those words represent concepts upon which you will base a lot of information. (They probably represent basic knowledge that students will need over time.)

- *Do teach fewer rather than more words.* But teach them more deeply. (Give students varied opportunities to process a few key words so they will understand a word's multiple dimensions and meanings.)

Don't's

- *Don't teach words just because the text says to.* (The list identified by the author or publisher may not contain the words your students should learn.)

- *Don't teach words students won't see or need again.* (Avoid wasting time teaching complicated proper names or place names.)

- *Don't select every italicized or boldface word.* (Make your own decisions about which words are essential for understanding. When key words aren't highlighted, you may have to find them yourself.)

- *Don't preteach every key word.* (Give students opportunities to use context, prior knowledge, and their own strategies to learn new words independently.)

Finally, DO remember . . . to teach new words not just before reading, but also during and after reading!

Figure 3.5 *Follow these tips when you teach vocabulary.*

3. Determine when to teach new words. It is a good idea to vary *when* you teach vocabulary. Sometimes it makes sense to teach a few key words *before* reading that are critical to comprehension. However, sometimes it makes sense to teach new words *after* reading. When students meet new words *during* reading, they can practice their word-learning strategies independently of you. Then you can assess whether their strategies worked and, if necessary, teach new vocabulary after reading. In fact, it is often a good idea to spend time after reading developing the multiple dimensions of a word.

4. Activate students' schema and build metacognition. When students store specific words (new information) by linking it to their existing schema (their network of organized information), there is a better chance they will remember the new word later. So, always try to connect the new with the known. Be sure to practice this procedure with students, pointing out to them how it helps them learn new words, and have individual students share with the class how it works for them. This builds a metacognitive skill that will serve students well when they are trying to learn new and difficult words and information.

5. Teach students to use context. Help students use context to figure out the specific meaning of a word. Teach them to use the pictures and/or graphics that accompany text and the words in a sentence that surround an unknown word, Emphasize that the sentences within a paragraph often give clues to a word's meaning. There are many different ways to show students that context can help them as they try to unlock difficult words (see Figure 3.6). The use of context is included in the questions on page 53 to help decode hard words, and answering them can provide students with reasonable guesses about unknown words.

CONTEXT

- *Picture:* Look at the picture for a clue: She wore a bridal *veil.*
- *Definition:* Sometimes the word is defined in the same sentence: The bride was *attired,* or dressed, in a white gown.
- *Series:* Commas signal that there are some words that may mean the same thing: The bride and groom joined in the singing, dancing, eating, and *rejoicing.*
- *Synonym:* Sometimes a word's synonym follows in the next sentence: The bride was from Canada, but the groom was from the United States. So they found a *site* between both countries. The location ...''
- *Antonym:* Sometimes a word that means the opposite, an antonym, comes in the next sentence: They didn't want to rush into a *quick* marriage, so they decided to have a lengthy engagement.''
- *Associations:* Think about what you already know: They got married while they were *aloft* in a helicopter flying above Niagara Falls.''

Figure 3.6 *Teach students a variety of ways to use context.*

6. Examine word structure. Teach word structure and relate new words to other words. The meaning of 60 percent of multisyllabic words can be inferred by analyzing word parts (Nagy & Scott, 2000). Students who know this are often more attentive to instruction in roots, prefixes, and suffixes. Knowing these word parts gives clues to what a word means. Since much of English comes from Greek and Latin, it is important to teach students the common derivatives. This is especially true in science and technology because these fields contain many multisyllabic terms.

Knowing just a few roots makes it much easier to figure out several other words that contain these roots. For example, students who know that *phil* means "love" can often infer the meanings of words that contain this root (e.g., *Philadelphia*: the city of brotherly love, *philanthropist*: one who loves people, *philatelist*: a lover of stamps, and *bibliophile*: a lover of books). You will read more about this important skill in Chapter 5.

7. **Teach for independence.** Model and teach word learning as an active strategy for independence by thinking aloud about the process you use. When you think aloud for students, you show them how you figure out a new word. One way to do this is to ask yourself the questions below while your students listen as you try to decode a difficult word. You can also encourage students to use these questions to unlock hard words. Then they can model their own word-learning strategies for one another.

- *Do the pictures/illustrations help?*
- *Are there clues in the surrounding print?*
- *How does the word start?*
- *Are there any chunks or parts I know?*

- *Is it like another word I know?*
- *What word makes sense here?*
- *What word looks right here?*
- *What word sounds right here?*

In Chapter 6, you will read more about fostering independence in word learning, because this is such an important aspect of building a large vocabulary.

8. **Provide guided practice.** Invite students to interact and collaborate around new words. Theory and research tell us that students need multiple opportunities to process and use new words in a variety of contexts to really learn them (Stahl & Fairbanks, 1986). Research also tells us that peer teaching promotes learning gains with a variety of learners, in multiple contexts, and across subject areas (Bromley, 2007). Not only do those who observe learn, but the peer teacher also learns because in order to teach well, he or she must know the material. Teaching requires a deeper understanding than learning does. Peer teaching also changes the traditional classroom context to create a community of learners in which all students share in the learning. Here are two ways to provide guided practice with words:

- *Mixed Groups:* You can form mixed-ability groups when you use reciprocal teaching (discussed on page 30) or when students are reading in other kinds of small groups. Mixing students with varying skills and abilities allows those with strong language and vocabulary skills to help those who lack vocabulary knowledge and do not understand words with multiple meanings. Other kinds of mixed groups are "interest groups" that allow students to work with others who have the same interests, or "gender groups" where boys work only with boys and girls only with girls. Variety in grouping gives all students opportunities to work with those who have the largest vocabularies and are most likely to be aware of more sophisticated language, know multiple meanings of words, and are probably able to share this knowledge.

- *Peer Teaching:* You can have students creatively peer-teach new words to one another in pairs or small groups before they begin a chapter or unit. Or, you can have each peer identify and list 3–5 important words (depending on the student's age and ability) after reading and then review their meanings and pronunciations with one another.

   Rules by Cynthia Lord (Scholastic, 2006) offers an opportunity for peers to teach words to each other. In this story, 12-year-old Catherine has an autistic brother, David, who uses word cards to communicate. His cards have been created by a therapist for typical situations, but David wants other words. So, Catherine makes him some new cards with words and phrases such as the following: *Awesome! Yeah, right. Whatever. Stinks a big one!! Sure. You bet!* Students in fourth, fifth, and sixth grades enjoy this story. After you read it aloud, have students work in pairs to identify words and make cards for other words they believe David might need or want. Ask students to teach these words to the class. Some sixth graders recently came up with these words: *dorky, cool, discouraged, alienated, normal.*

Offer Vocabulary-Building Activities

What's critical for all students, and especially struggling learners? Active engagement with the word and with other students helps them learn about the multiple aspects of a word in order to know the word well. When you engage students in a variety of ways to learn new words, rather than just telling them what a word means and pronouncing it for them, the chances of them really learning and remembering new words improve immensely.

Teach Words Directly

The discussion of wide and deep reading in Chapter 2, reading "to" students, is especially worth repeating here. I believe that reading aloud to students is one of the best ways to build their background knowledge. A good read-aloud invites students to make the connections that are a hallmark of reading comprehension: connections to self, connections to the text and other texts, and connections to the world. Students at all grade levels enjoy listening to stories and content selections being read to them. It builds their background knowledge, broadens their vocabularies, and deepens their concept knowledge.

Of course, when you read aloud, encourage everyone to ask questions and contribute to discussions as you clarify ideas, note usage and pronunciation, and point out multiple meanings when appropriate. Cunningham and Allington (2011) also suggest that a good read-aloud includes identifying and teaching no more than three difficult and/ or unique words. Teaching more words during a read-aloud may detract from students' enjoyment and understanding, so find the two or three words that will reappear in future reading and teach only those words.

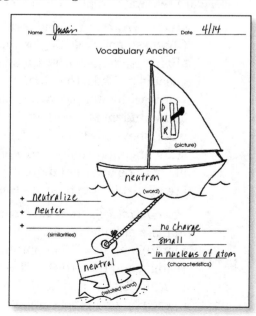

Figure 3.7

ACTIVITY ■ Vocabulary Anchor

Materials: Vocabulary Anchor reproducible (page 137), whiteboard, marker

When you begin a science unit, one of the new words you might need to teach is *neutron.* You could use a number of different graphic organizers, but I'll share one of my favorites here: the Vocabulary Anchor (Bromley, 2002; Winters, 2001). You can complete the Vocabulary Anchor on a whiteboard with input from your students.

The Next Step in Vocabulary Instruction © 2012 by Karen Bromley, Scholastic Teaching Resources

In the example in Figure 3.7, students anchored the new word *neutron* with the gearshift of a car, a word most knew well. When you have modeled the strategy for students, have each one choose a word that is troublesome for them and then work with a peer to make a Vocabulary Anchor or other graphic organizers to represent a word.

Extend Your Thinking

Why do you think the boat and anchor strategy helps students remember new words? Try it with a group of students and see what they think about it as a teaching tool.

ACTIVITY ▦ K-W-L (Know, Want to Know, Learned)

Materials: K-W-L graphic organizer, pens or pencils

K-W-L works effectively to introduce a new word because it taps students' prior knowledge first. Figure 3.8 shows how a group of fourth graders began a K-W-L chart for the new word *hydrofracking*. First, they listed what they already knew about *hydrofracking*. Next, they listed questions they had and what they wanted to know about the word. After reading the section, they list what they learned about the word. This strategy assesses students' prior knowledge and builds on it. Plus, it helps establish a purpose for reading: to find out what an unfamiliar word such as *hydrofracking* means.

K-W-L FOR *HYDROFRACKING*

K (What I know)	W (What I want to know)	L (What I learned)
• It is an action word because of the *-ing*. • It looks like *fraction*. • It has something to do with water because of *hydro-*. • It rhymes with *tracking*.	• Is it related to *fraction*? • Is it a math term or a science term? • Is it in the dictionary?	

Figure 3.8 *K-W-L draws on students' prior knowledge to help them learn a new word.*

ACTIVITY ▦ Chapter Titles

Materials: chapter books

This activity requires students to create their own titles for chapters in a book, using specific and, often, colorful vocabulary. They may use vocabulary from the story, or they may use nouns, verbs, synonyms, antonyms, or other descriptive words that characterize a particular chapter. First, have students look at the titles for each chapter in a book they have recently read. Ask them to identify titles they believe are especially good and brainstorm why (e.g., titles are usually short, inviting, don't tell too much, and contain words that grab our attention). Next, find a book you have read to students that does not have chapter titles. Then create some possible titles together. You can also have students do this in pairs or small groups.

Here are the titles third graders created for the first chapter of *Because of Winn-Dixie* by Kate DiCamillo (Candlewick, 2000).

- *"Bath Time"*
- *"Can We Keep Him?"*
- *"My New Friend"*
- *"Strangers"*
- *"Chaos!"*

Each title is appropriate and shows the variety of ways students responded to the first chapter. Their teacher added the last title, "Chaos!," as a way to share a new word and expand her students' vocabulary.

This activity develops vocabulary knowledge, comprehension, and creativity. You can discuss the words and titles students used and ask them to explain their decisions. This is a low-risk activity in which everyone can be right, as long as they support their ideas with reasons. Writing titles is motivating for struggling readers and writers since it requires writing only a few words. And you don't always need to use a book without chapter titles. Sometimes creating new titles is more effective when you use a book that already has chapter titles. In that case, challenge students to write better chapter titles than the author's.

ACTIVITY ▪ 160 Words in 3 Days

Materials: paper, pens or pencils, chart paper, and marker

Teaching in Action

Sandy, an ELL teacher, has his students work in groups for this activity, which builds reserves of nouns and verbs. He puts students in four groups and, on each of two days, he has each group make a list of 20 objects in the classroom (e.g., pencil, computer, desk, light switch, and so on). Next, Sandy has his students add a verb to each listed word that tells how to use the object (e.g., pencil writes, computer searches, desk stands, light switch turns on, and so on). In two days, the groups together have identified 160 words. On the third day, as the groups present their words to each other, Sandy writes the words on chart paper so students can see the words and share them orally.

There is bound to be a repetition of objects and words in this activity, which is good since struggling students need repeated exposures to learn words. This is an effective way to teach nouns as "words that name people, places, and things" and verbs as "action words." It builds vocabulary for common, ordinary classroom objects and words that show their function.

The Next Step in Vocabulary Instruction © 2012 by Karen Bromley, Scholastic Teaching Resources

ACTIVITY ■ Flag Compare

Materials: printed color images of the U.S. flag and flags of other nations (from a world atlas or a Web site, such as www.enchantedlearning.com), T-chart or Venn diagram, paper and pens or pencils

This activity helps recognize and celebrate the diversity in a classroom or school and, at the same time, builds on students' background knowledge.

Teaching in Action

For this activity, Sandy has his ELLs use the Internet to find and print color copies of the United States flag and the national flag of their country of origin. He says, "Students take notes in three categories: the colors on the flags, the shapes of the flags and the objects on them, and the meanings (or symbols) of the colors, shapes, and objects on the flags." Students write the words on Venn diagrams or T-charts to compare the similarities and differences between the two flags. Sandy continues, "Then, after giving students a topic sentence, I have them write a compare/contrast paragraph in three sections: the first two sentences compare the colors on the two different flags, the next two sentences compare the shapes and objects, and the last two sentences compare the meanings/symbols."

You can display the finished paragraphs with flag pictures on a bulletin board in your classroom or in the hallway for the rest of the school to see.

ACTIVITY ■ Pledge of Allegiance

Materials: a copy of the Pledge of Allegiance

You can use a copy of the Pledge of Allegiance to preteach students the meanings and pronunciation of difficult words like *indivisible, liberty, justice,* and so on. Then, as students learn to recite the pledge, they also learn the concepts for which the words stand.

Many teachers of struggling, uninterested students incorporate song lyrics, poetry, and rap lyrics into their teaching because of their unique appeal. Music and rhythm provide a special avenue that can build the vocabulary and comprehension of struggling learners.

Provide Guided Practice

Use the following ideas to provide guided practice with words. When you involve students in interacting together around new words, this active practice offers important experiences that build vocabulary. These collaborative activities may fit your students just as they are presented here, or you may adapt them to the specific needs of your students and curriculum.

ACTIVITY ■ Buddy Reading

Materials: a variety of books

This activity involves pairs of students reading books of their choice to one another. Oral reading to an audience provides practice in word recognition and builds the reader's fluency. It also promotes the listening comprehension and vocabulary development of the listener who may not be able to read the book independently. Buddy reading leads to better comprehension because students acquire many of the concepts they will encounter in subsequent reading. Bolstering students' vocabulary and conceptual knowledge through listening allows them to link this knowledge to new information in the printed text.

ACTIVITY ■ Journal Share

Materials: a notebook for each student, pens or pencils

Journal Share allows students to work together to share entries they have made in their vocabulary journals.

Teaching in Action

Paul has his sixth graders keep a social studies journal in which they list new words and draw simple pictures to represent the words. He says, "I tell them 'a picture is worth a thousand words.' I find it's a great motivator and a good way to teach difficult vocabulary. The students are eager to talk about their drawings and see how another person depicts the words. Sharing with each other helps them remember the words."

Figure 3.9

Peer sharing of vocabulary journals is another way to use collaboration and peer teaching to help reinforce the learning of new words (see Figure 3.9).

ACTIVITY ■ Song Lyrics

Materials: a copy of song lyrics for each student and a recording of its musical score

Teaching in Action

Many of Sandy's ELLs follow sports, especially baseball, so he uses song lyrics to show how learning words in context is superior to memorizing the definitions of unconnected words on a list. Sandy distributes lyrics from songs like "The Star Spangled Banner" and "Take Me Out to the Ball Game" to his students. Then he plays the songs themselves. Students sing along with the melody and follow the words in the lyrics. Sandy preteaches difficult words such as banner, spangled, perilous, *and so on to help with pronunciation and comprehension.*

The Next Step in Vocabulary Instruction © 2012 by Karen Bromley, Scholastic Teaching Resources

ACTIVITY ▩ I Have—. Who Has—?

Materials: index cards or paper, marker

This activity reinforces vocabulary that might be challenging for students (Bromley, 2002).

Teaching in Action

Katie, a fourth-grade teacher, often uses I Have—. Who Has—? after reading a book or a content chapter/unit. It can also be used before reading, as explained below.

1. *Choose words from a book or unit students have just read (identify as many words as there are students or repeat some of the difficult words so each student has a word).*

2. *Make index cards or half sheets of paper that read "I have_____." on one side and "Who has a word that means_____?" on the other side.*

3. *On each card or sheet, write a word on one side and the definition of a different word on the other side.*

4. *Tell students they will work together to create a vocabulary chain or circle.*

5. *Give each student a card and ask him or her to read both sides silently. Then call on a student to read the "I have" side of his or her card (the vocabulary word). Then have the same student turn over the card and read the "Who has?" side (the definition).*

6. *The student who has the matching "I have" card (vocabulary word) reads it. Then the student turns over his or her card to read the definition on the "Who has?" side.*

7. *The game continues until everyone has had a turn, and all the words have been reviewed.*

Katie's students love this game so much that they ask to play it every week. After students know how the game works, Katie has pairs or small groups create the word cards for particular books and/or content units.

ACTIVITY ▩ Synonym Stretch

Materials: chart paper and marker

Many upper elementary and middle school teachers use the Synonym Stretch activity to expand students' vocabularies. Studying synonyms helps students become aware of the nuances of language and the multiple meanings of words.

On chart paper or a bulletin board, write a word that can be represented in many different ways, such as *house*. Challenge students to come up with synonyms, such as *abode, castle, casa, home, nest, hogan,* and *hole*. When students

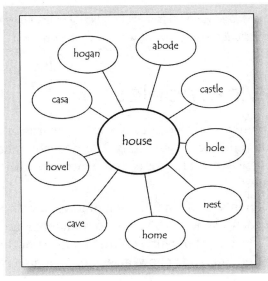

Extend Your Thinking

After reading Hoberman's book, see how many other houses students can brainstorm. Make a list on chart paper or a bulletin board of words and pictures that can help struggling readers and English learners.

Figure 3.10

have exhausted their store of synonyms, read them Mary Ann Hoberman's *A House Is a House for Me* (Viking, 1978), which contains 75 or more synonyms for *house*.

ACTIVITY ■ 3-D Words

Materials: paper and marker, 8-inch by 11-inch piece of tag board for each student or group, markers, classroom objects, glue

This activity requires students to research a word and teach it to a peer or their classmates (Bromley, 2002). It involves the visual and verbal modes and is useful after reading to reinforce and review key vocabulary, while also promoting the use of the dictionary, Internet, and textbooks. Follow these directions:

- Select key words and write each on a slip of paper.
- Give each student or each team a piece of tag board. Have each student or team draw a picture of the word.
- Tell students to write the word and a definition, using real objects to make the word three-dimensional, and use the word in a sentence.
- Ask students or groups to teach one another their words using their 3-D display.
- Make copies and collate in a Team Words book for each student.

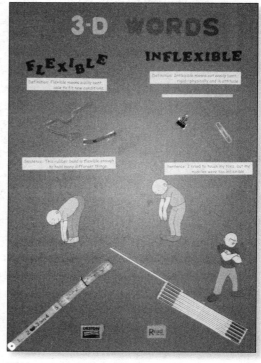

Figure 3.11 *When students create and teach 3-D Words together, the words "stick." (courtesy of Karen Antikajian)*

Teaching in Action

In addition to using individual words, Kira finds her third graders enjoy creating 3-D displays for words and their opposites. Kira has her students share them with each other as well as with younger students (see Figure 3.11).

ACTIVITY ■ Mnemonics

A mnemonic is a memory tool—a special word or words or a poem that helps a person remember something. Many teachers help students commit new words and concepts to memory with the following techniques:

- **Acronym:** an invented combination of letters, with each letter acting as a cue to an idea you need to remember. *Example:* In ROYGBIV, each letter represents an element of the color spectrum—red, orange, yellow, green, blue, indigo, violet.

Extend Your Thinking

What other mnemonics have you learned? What techniques have you heard other teachers use to help students remember new words or difficult concepts?

The Next Step in Vocabulary Instruction © 2012 by Karen Bromley, Scholastic Teaching Resources

- **Acrostic:** an invented sentence where the first letter of each word is a cue to an idea you need to remember. *Example:* The acrostic Every Good Boy Deserves Fun helps us remember the order of notes in the treble clef: E, G, B, D, F.
- **Rhyme:** a rhyming poem that acts as a cue to an idea you need to remember *Example:* The rhyme "30 days hath September, April, June, and November. All the rest have 31, save February" helps us remember the number of days in each month.

Try Independent Activities

Today there are more and more electronic books available online for students to read. Electronic books often motivate uninterested students because these books are animated, they include sound narration and allow the reader options to stop and start the reading at will. Here are some suggestions to explore.

ACTIVITIES ■ E-Books

Materials: computer with Internet access

- **BookPALS Storyline:** On the Internet, bookmark an online set of videos where students of all ages can enjoy literature read aloud by well-known actors (www.storylineonline. net). Listening to stories and seeing people read them aloud builds students' prior knowledge, adds new vocabulary, and exposes them to text they might not normally read.

- **TumbleBook Library:** This online collection contains animated, talking picture books and chapter books (www.tumblebooks.com/library/asp/about_tumblebooks.asp). The pages of each book turn themselves and are narrated. A student can turn this feature off and proceed to read orally at his or her own speed and then discuss the text with a friend or the teacher.

- **International Children's Digital Library:** This site was created by an interdisciplinary team from the University of Maryland and Internet Archives (http://en.childrenslibrary. org). It contains unabridged books, published in many languages, that have received some type of recognition in their country of publication. Students can access this site and choose books to read independently or with a partner in school or at home.

ACTIVITY ■ What's New?

Materials: computer with Internet access

Pair students (one who has keyboarding and computer skills and one who lacks them or is developing these skills) to do an Internet search on "new words in the dictionary." They should be able to find words like those in Figure 3.1 on page 46. Guide students to www.merriam-webstercollegiate.com/info/new_words.htm, which includes the definition, pronunciation, function, and etymology of new words that student partners can share with the class.

Also, encourage students to bring in and share new slang that they hear used outside school. This is another way of demonstrating to students that English grows and changes regularly. Then share the class's collaborative work by having students make a bulletin board display of the words they discovered.

Daily Calendar: Immigration

This calendar contains activities that require research on the Internet. First, you might want to discuss the calendar's topic—immigration—and help students understand that many of our parents, grandparents, or great-grandparent are or were immigrants. You might also want to read and discuss books such as the following with your class:

- *Coming to America: The Story of Immigration* by Betsy Maestro (Scholastic, 1996). This book tells the story of Cuban immigrants fleeing their country to begin a new life in the United States.

- *If Your Name Was Changed at Ellis Island* by Ellen Levine (Scholastic, 1993). Levine documents the immigration procedures followed at Ellis Island between 1892 and 1914. The book offers answers to questions such as, "What did people bring with them?"; "What happened if you were detained?"; and "How did people learn English?"

- *I Hate English!* by Ellen Levine (Scholastic, 1989). This book helps both English speakers and ELLs understand what goes on in the minds of some immigrant children who are learning English.

- *The Memory Coat* by Elvira Woodruff (Scholastic, 1999). Woodruff tells the story of a coat worn by an immigrant child that the author viewed at the Ellis Island Immigration Museum.

You can send this calendar or parts of it home for parents to use, or use it yourself in your classroom to extend students' vocabulary on the topic of immigration. From these activities, students can learn the following words and concepts: *immigration, emigration, citizen, green card, visa, naturalized citizen, pilgrim,* and *passport.*

DAILY CALENDAR: IMMIGRATION

Week 1: Getting Started

1. **In a dictionary,** look up the meanings of *immigration* and *emigration.* How are these words the same and how are they different? Make up a special way to remember what they mean and how to spell them.

2. **Go to the library** and borrow *Coming to America: The Story of Immigration* by Betsy Maestro (Scholastic, 1996) or another picture book about immigration. Read it to find out why the message is important to all Americans.

3. **Look up the word** *citizen* and find out what it means. Are you a citizen of the United States or another country? What rights and responsibilities do you have as a citizen? At what age does someone become a citizen?

4. **Interview an adult** who is a citizen of the United States. Find out what rights and responsibilities this person has. At what age can a citizen vote?

5. **Did you know** we are all descended from immigrants? Ask your parents or grandparents about your family's first relatives who immigrated to the United States. Find out who they were, where they came from, and where they settled.

Week 2: Understanding Immigration

6. **With a friend**, read the book *Immigrants* by Martin Sandler (HarperCollins, 2000). Look closely at the pictures (over 100 of them) and talk about how it might feel to leave your home and go to a new place to live.

7. **Do you know** any immigrants, or are you an immigrant? Interview someone who has immigrated recently to the United States. Find out why they immigrated and what is hard about being an immigrant. Find out about his or her family, favorite foods, and so on.

8. **Make a Venn diagram** and compare yourself with the person you interviewed. What do you have in common? Write these things in the center where the two circles overlap. What are your differences? Write each of your names in one of the circles and jot down ways in which you differ from each other.

9. **With a friend**, read the book *Angel Child, Dragon Child* by Michele Surat (Scholastic, 1989). Talk about these questions: Why did the principal tell Raymond to write Ut's story? Do you think it was a good punishment? Explain why or why not.

10. **Make a prediction** about why the main character in *I Hate English!* by Ellen Levine (Scholastic, 1999) doesn't like the English language. Read the book to find out if you need to change your prediction or whether you were right.

Week 3: Exploring Immigration

11. **A quilt** can tie the lives of family members together and be a symbol to them. Read *The Keeping Quilt* by Patricia Polacco (Simon & Schuster, 2001) and find out what this homemade quilt symbolizes for this family.

12. **What is** a *green card*? Use the Internet to search this term by typing "green card" in the search window. Then go to www.immigrationsupplies.com to find information on the Green Card Program, visas, and citizenship.

13. **What is** a naturalized citizen? At the same Web site you visited yesterday, find out how an immigrant can become a naturalized citizen. Then tell someone about it.

14. **What does** INS stand for? Go to Acronym Finder at www.acronymfinder.com. Then do a search on the term to see what job this government agency does. Tell whether you would want to work for the INS.

15. **Find Ellis Island** and the Statue of Liberty on a map of New York City. Did you know that France gave us "Lady Liberty" to symbolize our freedom and liberty from England? Do you know when they made this gift to us?

Week 4: Exploring Further

16. **Read** *Ellis Island: New Hope in a New Land* by William Jay Jacobs (Simon & Schuster, 1990). What were some of the hardships and problems new immigrants had? Why did America feel so much like a home for them?

17. **Read** *Lupita Mañana* by Patricia Beatty (HarperCollins, 2000). Why did Lupita and Salvador make the dangerous journey to cross the border from Mexico to America?

18. **With a friend**, look up the word *pilgrim* in the dictionary. Is a pilgrim the same as an *immigrant*? Talk about the differences and decide together what sets them apart.

19. **Borrow the video** (Phoenix Learning Group, 2008) or book *Molly's Pilgrim* by Barbara Cohen (Morrow, 1998). With a friend, watch the video or read the book. How did Molly's mother help Molly and the teacher understand what a pilgrim really is?

20. **With a friend**, take turns reading the questions and answers in the book *If Your Name Was Changed at Ellis Island* by Ellen Levine (Scholastic, 1994). Take turns reading the interesting quotes by both children and adults.

Week 4: Extending Yourself

21. **Read** *A Picnic in October* by Eve Bunting (Harcourt, 1999) to find out why the main character's grandmother insists that the family visit Ellis Island each year to celebrate Lady Liberty's birthday.

22. **Look at a map** of the Caribbean Sea and read the book *How Many Days to America?* by Eve Bunting (Clarion, 1988). Where do you think these people came from? (Hint: It's a Caribbean island.) Are they legal or illegal immigrants? What may happen to them? Do you agree with this outcome?

23. **Thanksgiving means** many things to many different people. With a friend, list all the things Thanksgiving means to you and all the things it might mean for immigrants to the United States.

24. **Work with a friend** to list all the reasons people emigrate from one country to another and all the problems they might have. You should have at least five reasons for each.

25. **Call the Chamber of Commerce** or the mayor's office to find out what special things your community does for newcomers. First write down your questions, and then tell them who you are and what you want to find out. Be ready to take notes.

Week 5: Reaching Out

26. **Interview your school's principal**, a classroom teacher, and an ELL teacher. Find out how your school helps immigrants. What special programs or events help immigrants?

27. **Call the post office** to find out what a passport is and how to get one. Ask if you need one to travel to Mexico or Canada, our two closest neighbors. Will you ever need a passport? How much does a passport cost? How long do they last? Be ready to take notes.

28. **How could** you and your friends help a new immigrant who moves to your community and enrolls in your school or church? Put yourself in his or her shoes and think about how you would feel. Be creative and think of things you and your classmates can do.

29. **Ask your PTA** or PTO to organize an International Dinner for your school. Get your friends to volunteer to help. You can send invitations to everyone asking them to bring a dish from their native culture or country.

30. **Make a poster display** to show what you have learned about immigration. Use color pictures and neat printing to make it inviting. Share this project with your family and then ask your teacher if you can share it with your classmates.

CHAPTER 4

Looking Closely at Word Structure

"In reality, morphology (word parts) and information gained from context and pictures are used together to figure out new words."

"Get your students into the habit of looking at an unfamiliar word and asking the question: Do I know any of the word parts?"

(Cunningham, 2009; pp. 40, 41)

Many elementary school teachers believe that morphology instruction is best left to the middle grades, but these teachers misunderstand morphology. Remember that morphemes are the smallest meaning units of language (see Chapter 1). Thus, morphology is the study of how letters go together to represent meanings. Also, remember that graphemes are individual letters that may be joined in ways that hold no meaning (blends and letter clusters).

Basic morphemic knowledge needs to be taught beginning in the early elementary grades. For example, the Common Core State Standards (2011) suggest that beginning in grade 2, students should recognize and be able to "use the most frequently occurring inflections and affixes as a clue to the meaning of an unknown word" (e.g., *-ed, -s, re-, un-, pre-, -ful*); in grade 3, students should be able to "use a known root word as a clue to the meaning of an unknown word with the same root" (e.g., *company, companion*).

This chapter will help you analyze and teach word parts, but it is organized a bit differently from previous chapters. The aspects of word structure (both meaningful and non-meaningful) that you need to know in order to teach them well are discussed, and I provide ideas in each section for activities that often begin with direct instruction and conclude with guided practice.

Word Parts and Morphology

Readers decode words by looking at *word parts that do not have meaning* (onsets, rhymes) and at *word parts that hold meaning* (inflectional endings, affixes, and base words or roots) (see Figure 4.1 on page 67). Of course, the most elementary part of a word is a letter. Single letters, blends, digraphs, and letter clusters do not hold meaning. However, once young children and struggling readers learn the letters of the alphabet, they can begin to recognize the onsets and rhymes that together make the phonograms you read about in Chapter 1. Then the sight vocabularies of students increase as they gain the ability to substitute onsets (initial consonants, blends, and digraphs) to make rhyming words or word families. So, recognizing both phonograms and compound words is a good way for beginning readers to develop awareness of word parts.

BEST BOOKS AND ARTICLES ON VOCABULARY LEARNING

You will find many ways to teach word structure to students at a variety of grade levels in the professional books listed below. Also, be sure to read related articles in journals like *The Reading Teacher, Journal of Adolescent and Adult Literacy, Language Arts,* and *Teaching Exceptional Children,* and visit Web sites such as www.readwritethink.org co-sponsored by The International Reading Association (IRA) and The National Council of Teachers of English (NCTE).

- Allen, J. (2007). *Inside words: Tools for teaching academic vocabulary Grades 4–12*. Portland, ME: Stenhouse.

- Bear, D. R., Invernizzi, M., Templeton, S., & Johnston, F. R. (2011). *Words their way: Word study for phonics, vocabulary, and spelling instruction* (5th ed.). Upper Saddle River, NJ: Pearson.

- Beck, I. L., McKeown, M. G., & Kucan, L. (2002). *Bringing words to life: Robust vocabulary instruction.* New York: Guilford.

- Blachowicz, C., & Fisher, P. J. (2002). *Teaching vocabulary in all classrooms* (2nd ed.). Upper Saddle River, NJ: Merrill-Prentice Hall.

- Block, C. C., & Mangieri, J. N. (2006). *The vocabulary-enriched classroom: Practices for improving the reading performance of all students in grades 3 and up.* New York: Scholastic.

- Cunningham, P. M. (2009). *What really matters in vocabulary: Research-based practices across the curriculum.* Boston: Pearson.

- Cunningham, P. M., & Allington, R. L. (2011). *Classrooms that work: They can all read and write* (5th ed.). Boston: Allyn & Bacon.

- Fisher, D., & Frey, N. (2008). *Word wise and content rich: Five essential steps to teaching academic vocabulary.* Portsmouth, NH: Heinemann.

- Fox, B. J. (2012). *Word identification strategies* (5th ed.). Boston: Pearson.

- Rasinski, T., Padak, N., Newton, R. M., & Newton, E. (2008). *Greek and Latin roots: Keys to building vocabulary.* Huntington Beach, CA: Shell Education.

- Scott, J. A., Skobel, B. J., & Wells, J. (2008). *The word-conscious classroom: Building the vocabulary readers and writers need.* New York: Scholastic.

- Templeton, S., Bear, D. R., Johnston, F., & Invernizzi, M. (2010). *Vocabulary their way: Word study with middle and secondary students.* Boston: Pearson.

Extend Your Thinking

How would you go about drawing students' attention to the compound words and multisyllabic words in these books and learning them?

WORD PARTS AND MORPHOLOGY

Word Part	Definition	Examples
Onset	A letter or letters that begin a word	b-, l-, r-, cl-, str- , ch-, sh-, th-, wh-
Rhyme	A group of letters (a phonogram) that makes a word when coupled with onsets or initial letter(s)	-ill, -ake, -ant
Inflectional ending	Final letters added to words	-s, -ed, -ing
Compound word	Two words that make one word	butterfly, snowman, classroom, playground
Prefix	A word part added at the beginning of a root	re-, un-, pro-
Suffix	A word part added at the end of a root	-er, -est, -tion
Root	A base word to which affixes can be added	duct, act, aud
Word families	Rhyming words OR words that share a common meaning unit	cake, lake, sake react, transact, action
Cognate	A word that shares the same ancestry and meaning with another word	action, *acción*

Figure 4.1 *Some word parts hold meaning, and some do not.*

Compound Words

Cunningham (2009) suggests that compound words are a good way to begin teaching morphology because many commonly used English words are compounds. So, when first-grade teachers teach young students to put words like *snow* and *man* and *butter* and *fly* together to make *snowman* and *butterfly*, they are teaching students to look for meaningful parts of words. When first-grade teachers teach young students about word endings like *-s, -ed,* and *–ing*, they are also teaching morphology.

Teaching young children and struggling students to look for word parts in long words is a good way to help them become independent word solvers, too.

Teaching in Action

To this end, Allison, a first-grade teacher who reads often to her class, uses these opportunities to make her students aware of compound and multisyllabic words. Here are three books she reads to her class at the beginning of the year and some of the multisyllabic words they contain:

- Johnny Appleseed *by Jodie Shepherd (Scholastic, 2010):* hundred, Chapman, Massachusetts, Elizabeth, stepbrothers, everything, orchard, thousands, seedling

- Galimoto *by Karen Williams (Mulberry Books, 1990):* cornstalks, something, angrily, plastic, policeman, murmured, afternoon, bamboo, ambulance

- The Sandwich Swap *by Queen Rania Al Abdullah and Kelly DiPucchio (Hyperion, 2010):* Salma, Lily, together, sandwich, surprised, triangles, applesauce, splattered

Here is an idea for guided practice with compound words in first and second grades.

ACTIVITY ◼ 1 + 1 = A Compound Word

Materials: 5-inch by 8-inch index cards, markers, pointer

Teaching in Action

Allison also creates a bulletin board in September with the title "Do I know my 1 + 1's?" Then, as children encounter compound words in their reading and writing, Allison has them write these words on cards and post them on the bulletin board. She encourages pairs of children during free time to use a pointer to point to individual words and practice pronouncing the words and using them in sentences. The collected words on the bulletin board are also a resource for children to use independently in their writing. As the year progresses and children learn the compound words, Allison removes some and adds new ones.

Onsets and Rhymes

In addition to developing an awareness of compound words, teachers of young children and struggling readers build their students' sight vocabularies with activities that involve categorizing words according to their graphic similarities. Activities that involve onsets and rhymes, or phonograms, build the sight vocabularies of first and second graders. Teach these word parts at the same time as you teach students about compound words.

When 37 "magic" phonograms (or rhymes) are paired with different onsets, over 500 words can be made (Blevins, 1998) (see Figure 4.2). Remember that onsets are the letters that begin words and that can make word families (groups of rhyming words) when they are coupled with rhymes or phonograms. The onsets usually taught in first grade that students need to know are the following:

- initial consonants
- consonant blends: *l, r, s* and three-letter clusters, such as *str* and *thr*
- consonant digraphs: *ch, sh, wh, th*

Here is an idea for young children, struggling readers, and English learners that builds knowledge of letter patterns and rhyming words as it increases sight vocabularies.

37 "MAGIC" PHONOGRAMS

ack	ay	ip
ail	eat	ir
ain	ell	ock
ake	est	oke
ale	ice	op
ame	ick	or
an	ide	ore
ank	ight	uck
ap	ill	ug
ash	in	ump
at	ine	unk
ate	ing	
aw	ink	

Figure 4.2 *These 37 "magic" phonograms make over 500 words.*

ACTIVITY ■ Word Sorts

Materials: index cards, markers, pictures from magazines and other sources, small plastic bags

Extend Your Thinking

How would you use this activity or adapt it to make it more effective?

Use word sorts initially to develop students' oral language and concept knowledge by showing them how to match pictures with words printed on cards that stand for the pictures (Bear, Helman & Woessner, 2009). If you include words from the phonogram list, such as *cat, hill, hand, plant,* and *tent,* you begin to help students learn basic Tier 1 sight vocabulary and become familiar with phonograms.

When students know the words, can pronounce them, and match them with pictures, you can take the activity one step further. Add words that rhyme with the pictured words (*cat, hat, rat; hill, bill, sill, still; hand, sand, stand,* and so on). For example, students can match the word *cake* with its picture and then find other rhyming words like *rake, sake, lake,* and *shake* and add them to the match. You can create plastic bags of 10–20 words and pictures so students can practice the sorts on their own or with a partner. This way of learning rhyming words improves struggling learners' phonics skills as well as their sight and meaning vocabularies.

Prefixes and Suffixes

There is substantial research and expert opinion supporting the notion that morphemic analysis should begin in the early primary grades (Bear, Invernizzi, Templeton, & Johnston, 2011; Moats, 2000; Mountain, 2005). In fact, Moats states, "Word structure at the morpheme level should be addressed as early as first grade" (2000; p. 74). She goes on to explain that "knowledge of roots and affixes facilitates rapid, efficient, and accurate reading of unfamiliar vocabulary" (p. 74).

So, along with onsets, rhymes, and compound words, affixes (prefixes and suffixes) play an important role in teaching vocabulary in the elementary classroom (see Figure 4.3 on the next page for the most common prefixes, roots, and suffixes).

Prefixes occur often in English, and they change the meaning of the base word to which they are attached. For example, when *un-* precedes *steady,* the meaning changes, resulting in *unsteady.* Young children quickly learn that the prefix *un-* means "not" and can begin to recognize it in words they hear in everyday conversations (*unhappy, unwilling, unlike, unwell*). Another prefix, *re-,* changes the meaning of base words to which it is attached. *Rewrite, rethink, redo,* and *replay* are words young children hear, and you can use these words to teach students that *re-* means "to do something over again."

Suffixes appear at the end of words, and they also change the meaning of base words. Suffixes like *-er, -est,* and *-tion* affect the part of speech of a word. In the word *walker,* the suffix *-er* changes a verb to a noun. In the word *tallest,* the suffix *-est* makes an adjective stronger, and the *-tion* in *invention* changes a verb to a noun.

Once students understand the meanings of prefixes and suffixes, the ripple effect takes place—this knowledge allows them to unlock the meanings of words they encounter in reading and, in turn, to use these words in their writing.

MOST COMMON PREFIXES

un- (not, opposite)	under- (too little)	pre- (before)	semi- (half)
re- (again)	in-, im- (in, into)	inter- (between, among)	super- (above)
over- (too much)	mis- (wrongly)	anti- (against)	mid- (middle)
in-, im-, ir-, il- (not)	non- (not)	en-, em- (cause to)	trans- (across)
dis- (not, opposite)	sub- (under)	ex- (out)	de- (away, from)
com- (together, with)			

MOST COMMON SUFFIXES

-s (plural)	-ible, -able (can be done)	-ity, -y (state of)	-ness (state of)
-ed (past tense)	-al, -ial (having characteristics)	-less (without)	-er, -or (person)
-ing (present tense)	-y (characterized by)	-en (made of)	-ion, -tion (act)
-ly (characteristic)	-ful (full of)	-ment (action)	-est (most)

COMMON LATIN & GREEK ROOTS

audi (hear)	spect (see)	graph (written, drawn)	scope (see)
dict (speak)	struct (build)	hydro (water)	tele (distant)
port (carry)	tract (pull, drag)	meter (measure)	ology (study of)
rupt (break)	vis (see)	scrib/script (write)	cred (believe)
auto (self)	bio (life)	photo (light)	

Figure 4.3 *Teach these word parts to help students unlock multisyllabic words.*

Mountain (2005) suggests three useful guidelines as you provide direct instruction in morphemic analysis:

1. When you teach a word, also gradually teach its derivative forms. To the word *plant*, add (and subtract) *-s, -ed, -ing, -er,* and *re-*.

2. When you teach an affix, introduce it with words that carry its most common meaning; present other meanings later. For the prefix *dis-*, start with the "not" meaning, as in *disagree*. Later, introduce the "reverse meaning," as in *disappear*.

3. When you teach a word that has meaningful parts, deconstruct and reconstruct the word with your students, pointing out the meaning of each part. For *unreachable*, show that the parts add up to the meaning "not able to be reached."

Here are some collaborative, guided practice activities for building an awareness of morphemic analysis and word parts in your beginning readers, as well as students at all grade levels who struggle with decoding and word recognition.

The Next Step in Vocabulary Instruction © 2012 by Karen Bromley, Scholastic Teaching Resources

ACTIVITY ■ Prefix Hunt

Materials: chart paper and marker

In this activity, you might introduce a prefix first graders need to know (like *un-*) and provide its meaning (e.g., *un-* means "opposite of" or "contrary to") (Berne & Blachowicz, 2008). Next, brainstorm with students a list of all the words they can think of that begin with *un-*. Then have students search the room, looking through all the print that is available, to find any other words that begin with the prefix. After a few minutes, gather students together and add any words to the list that they have found in the classroom. You can use the prefix scavenger hunt idea with suffixes to increase students' knowledge of suffixes as well.

ACTIVITY ■ Prefix "Splash"

Materials: newsprint or chart paper and marker, Prefix "Splash" reproducible (page 138)

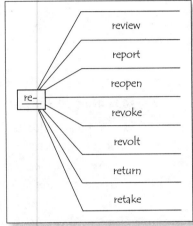

Encourage second- and third-grade students to brainstorm and collect words that begin with a prefix like *re-* and add them to a Prefix "Splash" chart (see Figure 4.4). Display the *re-* words that students find on a piece of newsprint, chart paper, or a bulletin board, and revisit these words occasionally. Have students use the words in sentences orally, and soon they will begin to use the words in their personal writing.

Figure 4.4 *This Prefix "Splash" activity teaches prefixes but works for suffixes, too.*

ACTIVITY ■ Suffix Web

Materials: chart paper and marker, dictionary

Draw a web on a bulletin board or chart paper with a suffix written in the center of it. Then help students brainstorm words that end with that suffix. Have students write their words outside the web and connect them to the center with lines or web strands. Students can use their dictionaries to find words that aren't in their speaking vocabularies. You can also create Prefix Webs and Root Webs with students to build their knowledge of these word parts.

ACTIVITY ■ Earthquake

Materials: small plastic bags, tag board cards, markers, scissors

Extend Your Thinking

What other activities and/or games have you used or seen that build students' awareness and use of prefixes and suffixes? What game could you create to encourage this kind of word learning?

Teaching in Action

To help her students recognize prefixes, Tami, a third-grade teacher, creates plastic bags containing 10–15 multisyllabic words that begin with common prefixes (e.g., undone, redo, into, prevent). She first prints these

words on tag board cards. Then Tami cuts the word cards apart, separating the prefix from its root or base (e.g., un- and done) and writes a sentence on the base card that contains the entire word. Tami's students like to shake the cut-up cards out of a bag and onto a desk or the floor. This disarray reminded children of an earthquake, hence the name of the activity. Once the cards are dumped out, students proceed to match the correct prefix with its base word, read the sentence printed on the back of the base word card, and use the new word in a sentence with a partner. Playing Earthquake with words containing suffixes also helps student recognize these word parts.

ACTIVITY ■ Chunking

Looking for chunks of letters in a difficult word is one way to help students unlock long words.

Teaching in Action

Tami, the third-grade teacher mentioned in the previous activity, models chunking for students by thinking aloud about a multisyllabic word as shown below:

"I met a long word this morning as I read the newspaper. The word uninterrupted appeared in a story about the rain and flooding in Pakistan." (At this point, Tami prints the word on the board so everyone can see it).

"To figure out the word, I looked for chunks of letters I know. I recognized un- at the beginning from the word unlike. I know that this prefix means "not." Next, I saw inter, and I thought about the intercom that connects the office with all the classrooms. Then I saw interrupt, and at the end I noticed -ed. Who knows what interrupt means? That's right, it means "to stop." Now, what do you think uninterrupted means? Yes, it means "without stopping." We did some good chunking to figure that word out. Has anyone met a hard word lately in reading? Can you tell us about how you used chunking to figure it out?"

ACTIVITY ■

Word Wheel

Materials: Word Wheel reproducible (page 139), pencil or pen, dictionary or thesaurus

A Word Wheel is a circle divided into sections. Filling in the sections of the circle (e.g., with words that give a definition, synonyms, antonyms, and so on), gives students the opportunity to dive deeper into a word's meaning and structure. You can assign a different spelling or

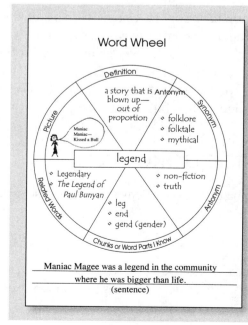

Extend Your Thinking

Try the Word Wheel to analyze the word *transformation* or with content-area words from a science topic. Does it help students learn the words? If so, how? If not, how would you change the Word Wheel to make it more effective?

Figure 4.5 *A Word Wheel helps students take a word apart and examine it deeply.*

The Next Step in Vocabulary Instruction © 2012 by Karen Bromley, Scholastic Teaching Resources

vocabulary word to each student or have several students complete one wheel together. Be sure to encourage students to use a dictionary or thesaurus. They can display their Word Wheels on a bulletin board after they share them with the group.

The Word Wheel in Figure 4.5 shows the word *legend*, which is found in *Maniac Magee* by Jerry Spinelli (Little, Brown, 1990).

Greek and Latin Roots

After taking three years of Latin in high school, I know that there are many Latin-based words in our everyday lexicon, and I realize that the roots of our language are Latin. But, when I read *Greek and Latin Roots: Keys to Building Vocabulary* (Rasinski, Padak, Newton, & Newton, 2008), I was surprised to learn the following things:

- 90 percent of English words with more than one syllable are Latin-based, and most of the remaining 10 percent derive from Greek.

- A single Latin root can generate 5–20 English words.

- Many science and technology terms that are added to English each year have Latin roots. For example, the term *cursor*, which is now part of computer lingo, has the same root as the word *course:* the Latin verb *currere*.

- 75 percent of Spanish is descended from Latin, so it should be easier for both English speakers learning Spanish and Spanish speakers learning English, because both languages share so many cognates.

These are good language facts for upper elementary and middle school teachers to know, especially content-area teachers, because most of the words in textbooks and materials students read have Greek and Latin roots. But classroom teachers, ELL teachers, and Spanish teachers can also benefit from a reminder of the origins of and similarities between the two languages.

When and how should you begin to teach Greek and Latin roots? Second and third grade is not too soon to teach roots and base words. Young students and struggling learners who recognize compound words are also ready to begin learning about base words and roots. Some teachers begin pointing out roots when they teach students to look for recognizable letter chunks. Other teachers realize the importance of self-selection and self-study to help students add multisyllabic words to their lexicons.

Nagy and Scott point out that "the meanings of 60% of multisyllabic words can be inferred by analyzing word parts" (2000). When a student knows what one word part means, this knowledge often unlocks the meanings of several other words. For example, if you know that *tele-* means "far or from afar," this knowledge can help you figure out the meanings of *television, telecommunication, teleprompter,* and *telegram*. Recognizing roots is extremely important as students enter the upper grades and middle school because content reading includes many technical and multisyllabic terms. And remember, knowing just one root can help your students unlock as many as 5–20 words.

Here are some ideas for providing a mixture of direct instruction and guided practice to students as you teach them about prefixes, bases, and suffixes.

Extend Your Thinking

How many words can you think of that contain these word parts: *-rupt* (to break: *erupt, rupture*); *-port* (to carry: *import, portable*); *-vac* (empty: *vacant, vacuum*)?

ACTIVITY ■ Divide and Conquer

Materials: chart paper and marker, students' Vocabulary Notebooks

This activity helps students recognize the structure, sound, and meaning of prefixes, suffixes, and bases (Rasinski, Padak, Newton, & Newton, 2008). Although *base* and *root* are often used to mean the same thing (I use them interchangeably), these researchers remind us that *root* is a generic term for any part of a word that holds meaning. So, prefixes, bases, and suffixes are all roots.

Begin the Divide and Conquer activity with a list of about ten words that have the same prefix (*unlock, unresponsive, unlikely, unpleasant, unrepentant, undo, unreal, unmade,* and so on), generated by you and your students. First, read the words orally with students and use the words in sentences. Then have students choose one or two words from the list and identify the base word(s) and what they mean. When students explain the word meanings, be sure to reinforce the idea that the meaning of the whole word is related to the meaning of the prefix and base together.

Have students list each complete word followed by its prefix, base, and root in their Vocabulary Notebooks or on a sheet of paper. Then ask them to give their own definition for each word. Here is a sample list:

Word	Prefix Base Suffix	Meaning
deflect	de + flect	to turn away
denounce	de + nounce	to speak against or disagree with
deplane	de + plane	to leave an airplane
promotion	pro + mo + tion	the act of moving forward

ACTIVITY ■ Greek and Latin Dictionaries

Materials: online Green and Latin roots dictionaries

There are many dictionaries of Greek and Latin roots that will help students infer the meanings of difficult, multisyllabic terms. Print a short dictionary of Greek and Latin roots for each of your students, like the one found at http://english.glendale.cc.ca.us/roots.dict.html. For each root or affix, this Web page provides an example word. Show students how to use it as a quick way to unlock terms like *pyromaniac* (crazy about fire: *pyr* means "fire" and *mania* means "madness"). Give students links to the Web sites below that can help them unlock difficult words more easily. Then hand out a list of multisyllabic words and have students determine their meaning using one of these online dictionaries:

- *http://wordinfo.info//words/index/info:* This site provides an alphabetical listing of word parts along with their definitions.

- *www.macroevolution.net/root-word-dictionary.html:* Here students can click on links to access pages of roots and affixes that often appear in biology and medicine.

- *www.etymologic.com:* This word game presents 10 randomly selected etymology or word-definition puzzles to solve. In each case, the word or phrase is highlighted in bold and a number of possible answers are given. Students choose the correct answer to score a point for that question.

ACTIVITY ■ Root Webs

Materials: chart paper and marker, dictionary, thesaurus

Select a root or have students choose one that has appeared recently or will appear in upcoming reading, such as *phil*. Print the root and its meaning in the center of a web, and invite students to add words to it that contain the root (see Figure 4.6). This is an authentic way to get students to use the dictionary and thesaurus. Then, when the web is complete and you have a few minutes before or after a lesson, you can ask students to choose a word from the web, give its meaning, and use it in a sentence. This practice helps cement the pronunciation and meanings of multisyllabic words in students' minds.

ACTIVITY ■ Root Trees

Materials: drawing paper and markers or colored pencils

This activity works especially well with words in science units. On a classroom wall or a bulletin board, display a sketch (or have a student do the sketch) of a tree trunk and branches, and write a root such as *meta-* on the tree trunk (see Figure 4.7). Have students draw leaves on the branches with related words and definitions on every leaf. Or, display a prefix on each branch and have students add leaves with words that begin with that prefix along with their definitions.

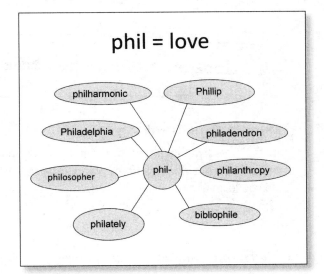

Figure 4.6 *Use a Root Web organizer to represent related words graphically.*

Figure 4.7 *A Root Tree collects words that grow from the same base word.*

ACTIVITY ■ Inspiration

Materials: computers with Internet access

Inspiration (www.inspiration.com) is a software program for K–12 students that serves as a visual way to explore and understand words, numbers, and concepts. The program includes Kidspiration for grades 1–5; Webspiration for grades 5–12; and Inspiration for Grades 6–12. It allows students to create graphic representations, outline, write, and make presentations. Each version connects to the Internet and lets students use clip art and pictures in their creations. Students can work together or individually to create graphic organizers as they explore roots and the words in which they occur (see Figure 4.8).

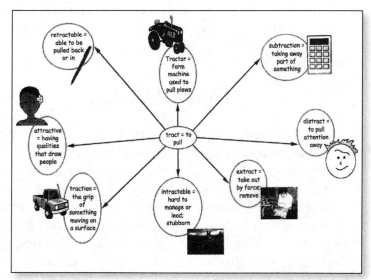

Figure 4.8 *Two seventh-grade students collaborated to create this organizer to explore the root* tract.

ACTIVITY ■ Word Pyramid

Materials: dictionary, thesaurus

A word pyramid builds students' abilities to parse multisyllabic words and explore the meaning of word parts. You can create a form for students to use, or they can make their own by drawing the appropriate blank lines. As the sample in Figure 4.9 shows, for the word *hemisphere*, students do the following:

- Write the word on the top line of the pyramid. (*hemisphere*)

- Write the component parts of the word on the next two lines. (*hemi sphere*)

- Write synonyms or words that define each component on the next four lines. (*half 50% round globe*)

- Write one or two sentences using the target word correctly on the last two tiers of the pyramid, with five and then eight words per line. (*The globe has two hemispheres.*) (*The equator separates the northern and southern hemispheres.*)

Figure 4.9

Extend Your Thinking

Try the Word Pyramid activity by creating a word pyramid yourself with the words *disagree* and *photograph*. What did you learn about these two words?

This activity nudges students to use the dictionary and thesaurus for a real purpose. It also enables you to reinforce correct spelling as students write the target word several times.

The Next Step in Vocabulary Instruction © 2012 by Karen Bromley, Scholastic Teaching Resources

ACTIVITY ■ Word Squares

Materials: chart paper and marker, Vocabulary Notebooks for students

This activity focuses on prefixes and roots to help students learn multisyllabic words (Hopkins & Bean, 1999). These authors found that this strategy helped develop the "independent problem-solving skills" of junior high and high school students in the Northern Cheyenne Reservation in Montana.

Begin by using a think-aloud to model Word Squares as you do the following:

- Draw a square and divide it into four smaller squares (see Figure 4.10).

- In the top-left square, write the prefix you want to teach.

- In the bottom-left square, write the dictionary definition of the prefix.

- In the top-right square, write a word that has the prefix and its definition.

- In the bottom-right square, draw a picture of that word.

Prefix	Defined	Root	Defined
sub-	submarine: a boat that goes under water	spect-	spectator: someone who watches but doesn't take part
under		watch or behold	
Definition	Drawing	Definition	Drawing

Figure 4.10 *Creating a Word Square connects students' prior knowledge to a new word.*

Students can copy your model into their Vocabulary Notebooks and use it to create their own Word Squares. You can give Word Squares as homework or a classroom assignment that students complete one or two days a week. Have students add their words to a list you post in the classroom to expose everyone to a range of multisyllabic words. Or, have students collect words that share the same prefix or root and post these lists in the classroom. Remember to tell students that the goal of this strategy is not just to help them learn the meanings of prefixes and roots but also to use this knowledge to figure out and learn new words on their own.

ACTIVITY ■ Flip-a-Chip

Materials: poker chips, markers, paper and pens or pencils, small plastic bags

This activity engages pairs of students in competition to build words from meaningful parts including prefixes, roots, suffixes, and inflectional endings (Mountain, 2002). While this interactive game is meant for older students, it can be used effectively with younger students, too. Flip-a-Chip is played with poker chips (stored in individual plastic bags) on which various prefixes and roots are written. For example, you might write *pro* on the front of one chip and *duce* on the front of another chip and then write *re* on the back of the *pro* chip and *voke* on the back of the *duce* chip. Then pairs of students can flip the chips and write all the words they can make as they put the two parts together (*produce, provoke, reduce,* and *revoke*). They can then add words they know to the *pro* list and the *re* list.

You can prepare other plastic bags with pairs of prefixes and roots, roots and suffixes, roots and inflectional endings, and encourage your students to play with these chips to make words. Innovative activities like these and the others described in this chapter can motivate students to learn how to unlock multisyllabic words. These activities can also be modified for younger students.

In fact, as I recommended at the beginning of this chapter, morphemic analysis should be taught to students in grades 1–3. When phonics and context don't help students unlock multisyllabic words, morphemic analysis often does (Mountain, 2005). This activity presents many ways to help young students unlock words. For example, the meaning of the word *tripod* may not be evident from pronouncing its two parts, *tri* and *pod.* The word's meaning may not be clear from reading a sentence where it is used in conjunction with the word *camera.* But, when you share words like *tricycle, triangle,* and *triceratops,* words students may already know that possess the chunk *tri,* the meaning of *tripod* may become evident.

ACTIVITY ■ Big Word Book

Materials: tag board or wall paper, markers, colored pencils, dictionaries, thesauruses, paper

This activity encourages students to compile all the multisyllabic words they are learning in a Big Word Book or Multisyllabic Word Book. Provide students with tag board or wallpaper for book covers, felt markers, colored pencils, dictionaries, thesauruses, and paper. Each page can hold one word, a drawing, and the word used in one or two sentences and/or a poem. Students might even divide their books into chapters—one chapter for three-syllable words, one chapter for four-syllable words, and so on. You might have students work together. As students are writing these books, they can read and review one another's pages to build their vocabularies. And, of course, sharing the completed books with other classes is a great way to build in real audiences.

Words From Other Languages

Three out of four words in the English dictionary have foreign origins. Many English words that derive from other languages are pronounced just as they are in the original language (Lederer, 1991), including *zoo* (Greek), *chandelier* (French), and *opera* (Italian). There is a "word tree" in the Ellis Island Museum in New York City that shows how English is actually a collection of words from many other countries. Each branch on the tree holds a word that we have imported from languages around the world (see Figure 4.11).

Figure 4.11 *Many English words come directly from the languages of other countries.*

Activities That Build on Similarities in Languages

Many words we share with other languages are not exactly the same in both languages, but are very similar. When two words have a similar origin and meaning, they are called *cognates*. Spanish and English are probably the best examples of languages that share ancestries and meanings (see Figure 4.12). Knowing this can help you teach English vocabulary to Spanish-speaking ELLs, and it can support your teaching of Spanish vocabulary to English-speaking students.

██

SIMILARITIES: SPANISH AND ENGLISH

- Many words are the same in Spanish and English (e.g., *adios, bonanza, cafeteria, corral, coyote, embargo, guerrilla, mesa, mustang, patio, renegade, silo, tomato, tortilla, vanilla*).

- Many English and Spanish words are cognates (*action/acción, coincidence/coincidencia, direction/dirección, evaporation/evaporación, fiction/ficción, industrious/industriosa, family/familia, fortunate/afortunado, nutrition/nutrición, preparation/preparación*).

Figure 4.12 *Spanish and English share many cognates.*

A trend I have noticed in children's book publishing is the release of books written in two languages. Two examples of such books are *Welcome to My Neighborhood! A Barrio ABC* and *Bienvenidos a Mi Barrio!* by Quiara Hudes (Scholastic, 2010); and *It's Christmas, David!* and *Lego la Navidad, David!* by David Shannon (Scholastic, 2010). Each of these "twin" books contains the same illustrations, but one is in English and the other is in Spanish. Making books like these available to students can help them in several ways. ELLs have their first language validated, and English-speaking students are exposed to another language. Students can read the books to one another in their native language, compare and contrast the two languages, and begin to appreciate and learn another language.

Other guided practice activities for building on similarities between languages to promote vocabulary growth and comprehension appear below.

ACTIVITY ▪

Writing in Two Languages

Materials: English dictionary and dictionaries in other languages, paper and pen

Having students write something in two languages, the one they know and the one they are learning, can build vocabulary in both languages.

Ask your students to translate a piece of writing in English into another language or vice versa, as Kayla, a sixth-grade student, did in the bio-poem in Figure 4.13. Kayla first wrote about herself in English and then translated her poem into Spanish. In the Spanish version, she used a Spanish name, Eva, to refer to herself. Activities like this build proficiency in the second language and can help students see similarities and differences between English and another language.

Pelo del bonde, ojos azules, más alto, y atletíca
Hermana de Ryan, hija de MaryAnn y George, amiga de la mayoría
Quien le encanta baloncesto, amigos, y familia
Quien se siente feliz, fantástico y magnífico
Quien necesita amar, amigos, y familia
Quien da amistad, amar, y honradez
Quien tiene miedo de las arañas, abejas y muerte
Quien le gustaría ver París, Londres, y Hawaii
Quien vive en Taylor, Pennsylvania

Blonde Hair, blue eyes, tall and athletic
Sister of Ryan, daughter of MaryAnn and George, friend to most
Who loves basketball, friends and family
Who feels happy, fantastic and magnificent
Who needs love, friends and family
Who gives friendship, love and honesty
Who fears spiders, bees and death
Who would like to see Paris, London and Hawaii
Who lives in Taylor, Pennsylvania

Figure 4.13 *Writing in two languages shows students the similarities and differences between the languages.*

ACTIVITY ■ Word Match

Materials: paper and pens

Before students read a story or book, give them an overview or summary of the material they will read. Also, create a list with at least ten important words from the story and distribute a copy to each student. Choose multisyllabic words or words that are Spanish-English cognates. Have students decide which words identify or relate to the setting, characters, theme, problem, and solution. Tell students to underline setting words, circle characters, check off theme words, and so on. Or, choose words that describe the main characters of the story and, after an initial description of the story, ask students to make guesses as to which words describe the main character(s). Students can underline words that describe one character, circle words for a second character, and so on.

Both variations of this vocabulary activity can improve comprehension. They engage students in making predictions about a story based on a small amount of evidence that you provide first. Be sure to encourage students to change their predictions as they read the story by returning to the underlined, circled, or checked vocabulary and making modifications. Then they learn that predictions can change as they gain new information.

ACTIVITY ■ Micro-Writing

Materials: paper and pens

This activity builds on similarities in English, specifically, knowledge of synonyms. It also simplifies writing for ELL and struggling students. *Micro* means "small," and the goal of this activity is to allow students to write book reports, character sketches, summaries, and so on using as few words as possible. It is a good way to encourage the use of synonyms, too. Begin with a model. First, write 6–8 words that describe you, for example, *teacher, leader, mother, runner, wife, cat-lover.* Next, have students describe themselves the same way. Then they can use the Micro-Writing activity to describe a character in a story they have read. For example, the words *Afghan, daughter, reader, writer, boy impersonator* describe Parvana, the main character in *The Breadwinner* by Deborah Ellis (Groundwood Books, 2003).

Extend Your Thinking

Use Micro-Writing to create a six-word biography of yourself as a vocabulary teacher and create an eight-word description of an exemplary classroom environment for word learning.

Micro-Writing lets students express themselves using a few key words and does not require them to use standard grammar, which is often difficult for ELLs especially. So, when writing is a challenge, beginning with just a few English words can be much easier than expecting students to write in complete sentences.

The Next Step in Vocabulary Instruction © 2012 by Karen Bromley, Scholastic Teaching Resources

How Does Spelling Fit?

Spelling contributes to vocabulary growth in two ways. First, seeing how individual letters go together to make a word helps students recognize those words and add them to their speaking and reading vocabularies. Second, when students can spell a word accurately, they know the word well, and their writing vocabularies grow. Thus, they "own" the word and can use it in their writing. Research supports this spelling-vocabulary connection. Studies show that exposing second and fifth graders to the spelling of new vocabulary words enhances their memory, pronunciations, and understanding of the meanings of the words (Ehri & Rosenthal, 2007). You can reinforce correct spelling for grades 1–6 students with guided practice in this activity.

ACTIVITY ▪ Spelling Cheerleading

Materials: chart paper and marker

This physical activity elicits visual, auditory, verbal, and kinesthetic responses by drawing students' attention to letter shapes and word structure (Rogers, 1999). Have students stand and "spell" words with their bodies by touching their toes for letters with descenders—letters such as *y* or *p*; stretching their hands above their heads for letters with ascenders—letters such as *d* or *b*, and putting their hands on their waists for letters that neither ascend nor descend, such as *a* or *o* (see Figure 4.14 for the body position of each letter). Tell your class to stand and cheerlead a list of words from the board or chart paper. You can have younger students cheerlead a list of words from two or three different word families, such as *-ame, -ape,* or *–and.* This helps them begin to sort words according to similar letter patterns. Older students can cheerlead important content-area words to help them learn and remember the spelling of this sometimes difficult vocabulary.

(b, d, f, h, k, l, and t) (a, c, e, i, m, n, o, r, s, u, v, w, x, and z) (g, j, p, q, and y)

Figure 4.14 *Physically representing letters builds spelling and word knowledge.*

Physically moving their body sensitizes students to how letters look in words. When students spell the words out loud together, this reinforces spelling patterns as well. Individual students also enjoy cheerleading a word for others to guess. When teachers use Spelling Cheerleading, they often discover improvement in students' spelling and recognition of word parts, as well as vocabulary growth. When I share Spelling Cheerleading with teachers and they use it with their students, they often report an improvement in students' legibility and appropriate letter formation. The visual aspect of this activity teaches students that some letters go below the lines on a sheet of paper, some sit on the lines, and some go above other letters.

Try Independent Activities

These activities move students toward independence in recognizing and using multisyllabic words.

ACTIVITY ■ Sparkling Words

Materials: bulletin board

Teaching in Action

Domenica, a fourth-grade teacher, keeps a bulletin board with the title "Sparkling Words" where she and her students post interesting multisyllabic words from their reading, such as consuming, elated, liberated, cacophony, exuberance, pandemonium, berated, vacate, proficient. Domenica encourages students to add new words to the board as they meet them, and she has students share with the class examples of how they use these words in their writing.

ACTIVITY ■ Multisyllabic Word Hunt

Materials: two 3-inch by 5-inch index cards for each student

Teaching in Action

Domenica also uses a Multisyllabic Word Hunt with her class to give students opportunities before reading to find word meanings on their own. Before her students read a chapter in George Washington's Socks by Elvira Woodruff (Scholastic, 1993), Domenica gave each student two index cards: Each card held a word and the page number where the word could be found in the text (e.g., concession, p. 45; bayonet, p. 43; allegiance, p. 63; ammunition, p. 44; rebellion, p. 50; authority, p. 53; arsenal, p. 60). She also listed the words on the board. Then, without revealing its meaning, Domenica introduced each word by pronouncing it and having students clap the syllables out with her. Next, she told students to find the words in the chapter and determine their meanings from the context. Domenica's goal was to build students' awareness of multisyllabic word structure and help them use context on their own to find the meaning of words. Before reading the chapter independently, students pronounced the words and shared their guess about their meaning.

Daily Calendar: Out of This World

The Internet provides many opportunities for students of all ages to learn new vocabulary independently in school or at home. Here, I suggest you use the ideas in this calendar to allow students to use what they have learned in school about word structure as they read and understand science material laden with multisyllabic words. The calendar can help students develop both electronic literacy and traditional literacy. In this collection of activities about astronomy and space, students will encounter these multisyllabic terms: *astronaut, aeronautical, innovation, exploration, intergalactic, endeavor,* and *discovery.* If families don't have Internet access at home, have students go to the local public library for free Internet access.

The Next Step in Vocabulary Instruction © 2012 by Karen Bromley, Scholastic Teaching Resources

DAILY CALENDAR: OUT OF THIS WORLD

Week 1: Getting Started

1. **Make a journal** and write everything in it you learn this month about astronomy and space. Use a spiral notebook or staple 10–15 sheets of paper together, number each sheet, and add a tag board or wallpaper cover. Decorate the cover and call it your Out of This World! Journal.

2. **Get a dictionary** and find out what *astronomy, astronomer,* and *aerospace* mean. Write the definitions in your journal.

3. **Find out** what an astronomer does. Read *Everything Kids' Astronomy Book: Blast into Outer Space with Stellar Facts, Intergalactic Trivia, and Out-of-This-World Puzzles* (Everything Kids Series) by Kathi Wagner and Cheryl Racine (Adams Media, 2008). What does *intergalactic* mean? Write new and interesting information and/or questions in your journal.

4. **Create a list** in your journal of all the small words you can make from the word *astronomer.* If you really challenge yourself, you should be able to make at least 25 words. (Maybe even 35 words!)

5. **Search the Internet** for information on the Kennedy Space Center. Where is it located? What is its history? What is its purpose today?

Week 2: Learning About the Solar System

6. **Write some questions** you have about the solar system in your journal. See if you can find answers to your questions in the book *Don't Know Much About the Solar System* by Kenneth Davis (HarperCollins, 2001). Write the answers in your journal.

7. **Go on a tour** of the planets with Ms. Frizzle in *The Magic School Bus: Lost in the Solar System* by Joanna Cole (Scholastic, 1992). How has the solar system changed since this book was written? How many planets are there? How many moons does each planet have?

8. **Look at the pictures** in *The Magic School Bus: Lost in the Solar System.* In this "story within a story," the text tells one story and the bubbles tell another one. If you enjoy this format, ask your teacher or library-media specialist for other books like it.

9. **Show a friend** how the earth *rotates* and *revolves.* Find a large ball to act as the sun and a smaller ball to be Earth and show these two movements. Draw a picture of *rotation* and *revolution,* show it to a friend, and explain the terms.

10. **Calculate the miles** between the sun and Earth. Light travels 186,000 miles a second, and a *light-year* is the distance light travels in one year. The sun is eight light-years away from Earth. How many miles from the sun is Earth?

Week 3: More About the Solar System

11. **Check your newspaper** to find out which planets are visible in the night sky this month. Where would you look for each one? Go outdoors with your family tonight and see which ones you can spot.

12. **Create an acrostic poem** for the words *solar system* or *astronomy.* Use words to describe feelings, sights, sounds, and things that relate to the word or words you choose.

13. **Visit NASA's Web site** (www.NASA.gov) and look for up-to-date information on the world's largest space-exploring organization. Keep notes in your journal and ask your teacher if you can share it with your class.

14. **Find out** how many space shuttles the United States has launched. When was the first one launched? What was it called? When was the most recent shuttle launch? What was the shuttle's name? Record this information in your journal.

15. **Find the meanings** of *comet, meteor,* and *asteroid.* Use a dictionary or read *Far-Out Guide to Asteroids and Comets* by Mary Kay Carson (Bailey Books, 2010). Write the definitions and draw a picture of each on a separate page in your journal.

Week 4: Beyond the Solar System

16. **Search the Internet** to find out who Galileo was and why he was important. You can also read *Starry Messenger: Galileo Galilei* by Peter Sis (Farrar, 1996). Why do you think this book is a Caldecott Honor book?

17. **Visit www.stsci.edu**, the Space Telescope Science Institute's homepage. Find out what the Hubble space telescope is and look at images of its amazing findings. Make notes in your journal of new and interesting things you learned.

18. **Write a letter** to the Amateur Astronomers Association (1010 Park Ave., New York, NY 10028). Find out how to join and share this information with your science teacher and your classmates.

19. **Find a space club** near you by using the Internet and entering the phrase "astronomy clubs" in a search engine. Find out what they do and how someone can join. Share this information with your science teacher and classmates.

20. **Do you know** the difference between *planetarium* and *observatory*? How can you find out? Try searching the Internet and make notes in your journal. Check the telephone book to see if there is a planetarium or observatory near you and visit one or both.

Week 5: Exploring More Space

21. **Create your own space song** by making new verses for "Twinkle, Twinkle, Little Star." Here's an example to get you started: "Blast off, blast off, little rocket . . ." Sing your song to a friend.

22. **Find a magazine** in the library like *Highlights* or *Discovery* and look for articles on astronomy or space. Look at the pictures and captions first to see what you can learn and then read the articles.

23. **The Milky Way** is a candy bar, but it's also something else . . . a galaxy. Read *Planets, Stars, and Galaxies: A Visual Encyclopedia of Our Universe* by David A. Aguilar (National Geographic, 2007) or search the Internet for the term and write a short paragraph in your journal explaining what a galaxy is. Read it to a friend.

24. **Find the bears** in the sky with a friend by investigating the words *stars* and *constellation* on the Internet or in *The Usborne Complete Book of Astronomy and Space* by Lisa Miles and Alastair Smith (Scholastic, 1998).

25. **Draw pictures** in your journal of the constellations called Ursa Major (the Great Bear) and Ursa Minor (the Little Bear). Label each star with its name. In which constellation is the North Star located? Go outdoors at night with your family and see if you can find these two constellations in the sky.

Week 6: Keep on Keeping on . . .

26. **Go online** and visit *The Wired Owl,* a science magazine, at www.owlkids.com. Look for any articles on astronomy or space to see what else you can learn.

27. **Go to** www.pbs.org/wnet/hawking/html/home.html to find out about Stephen Hawking, perhaps the most brilliant scientist since Einstein. He is best known for his work on black holes. Make notes in your journal and write a short biography. Ask your parents or teacher to help you revise it and then ask to share it with your classmates.

28. **Reread your journal entries** and think about what you have learned this month. Create a poem, an acrostic, a project, a report, a song—something to bring together all you know now that you didn't know when you began these activities. Name your project Out of This World! and share it with your parents, teacher, and classmates.

 The Next Step in Vocabulary Instruction © 2012 by Karen Bromley, Scholastic Teaching Resources

CHAPTER 5

Creating Independent Word Learners

"Vocabulary is just as important in art class as it is in social studies or science. I want students to know the words for the techniques they are using. When I introduce terms like 'cross-hatching' or 'tessellation,' I put the words on the whiteboard so students can see them, and I show examples. We look at the crosshatching in Maurice Sendak's Where the Wild Things Are. *To learn about tessellation and symmetry, we study M. C. Escher's drawings on the Web at www.mcescher.com. Then I step back and let students talk. I ask them to share their impressions about what they saw. I am really happy that my weak readers latch onto these words and use them with each other as they practice a particular style."*

—Sarah, a middle school art teacher

To help students learn important art vocabulary, Sarah encourages them to examine various models. She wants students to know and use the terms for what they are doing in art class. Sarah believes that learning content-specific words like *crosshatching, tessellation*, and *symmetry* gives students confidence and empowers them to be successful in school. She demonstrates various styles and techniques for students and encourages their interactions around the new words. Sarah believes that active involvement helps all students become independent word learners, but especially struggling readers.

This chapter provides activities to build students' independence in learning content-specific words, English Language Arts (ELA) vocabulary, and testing terms. I include a variety of activities that give students opportunities to engage with one another, some that involve direct instruction, and some that provide guided practice. You will find that some activities work best for teaching content-area terms, while other activities are more generic and useful for teaching all types of vocabulary.

There Is No "Silver Bullet"

In Chapter 1, I discussed the need to rethink our vocabulary regarding teaching and word learning. There are several reasons for this. First, many teachers teach vocabulary using such flawed approaches as "assign, define, and test" and "identify, discuss, and assume."

Second, many of the instructions in the basal readers and content texts that many teachers use are mechanical and do not consider what students know and need to know. In addition, many of these activities are not rich and/or varied enough to result in word learning. Third, just providing definitions and using discussion to teach new words is not nearly enough to allow most students to really learn new words well. Fourth, many teachers believe that students can learn new words from context. These teachers don't realize that they need to teach students *how to use* context to decode words, or that context itself is not always enough.

Guess what? Even though we want to find the magic silver bullet that provides a quick and easy answer to the problem, there is no silver bullet or best method for teaching vocabulary. We know that just seeing a word several times doesn't translate to learning that word well. We know that just providing a word's definition doesn't mean the word will be learned well. We know that word learning is different for each student, and one size doesn't fit all. Just as there is no best method for teaching vocabulary, there is no best way to learn words or become an independent word learner. In fact, students vary tremendously in the ways they learn. What we do know is that strategies and activities that include definitions, associations, using context, and active engagement in meaningful learning are most effective. So, we need to be mindful of this and offer a menu of opportunities for building and stretching students' vocabularies and independence.

Building Independence

The Common Core State Standards (www.corestandards.org) state that students should be able to "demonstrate independence in gathering vocabulary knowledge when encountering an unknown term important to comprehension or expression." Thus, involving students in the kinds of activities you will read about in this chapter (and have read about in this book) extends their ability to unlock and understand long words. With good vocabulary teaching, you can achieve your ultimate goal, which is to help students transfer their learning and become independent word solvers.

The Common Core State Standards also state that students should be able to "acquire and use accurately a range of general academic and domain-specific words and phrases sufficient for reading, writing, speaking and listening." These words are necessary for learning across the curriculum, and they are often multisyllabic and difficult because the concepts are unknown and/or abstract.

Teachers often think of these "academic and domain-specific words" as content-specific vocabulary or Tier 3 words. Tier 3 words (e.g., *albatross, peninsula, nucleus*) are rare and sophisticated, and have meanings specific to a content area. Tier 2 (e.g., *absurd, fortunate, merchant*) words are important and appear frequently across content areas and ELA texts. Tier 1 words (e.g., *happy, baby, cat, walk*) are basic high-frequency words that most students recognize on sight. Remember that teaching Tier 2 and Tier 3 words means focusing on fewer rather than more words and teaching words in depth as you connect to students' background knowledge through definitions, associations, word parts, and morphology. (Beck, McKeown & Kucan, 2002).

Harmon (2002) suggests ways to develop your students' independence in learning words that appear in materials across the curriculum in science, social studies, math, and ELA. These strategies include figuring out the purpose of the word, finding out what clues are in the sentence, looking before and after the sentence, and studying the word.

The Next Step in Vocabulary Instruction © 2012 by Karen Bromley, Scholastic Teaching Resources

Teach Reflection

Students also need to take ownership and make connections that allow them to use a strategy in the future, so encourage reflection by having students ask themselves the following questions:

- *What did I learn today about figuring out the meaning of new words?*
- *What is the most important thing I learned today?*
- *How can this help me when I read on my own?*
- *What can I do now when I meet a new word as I read on my own?*

Ashley, age 10, reflected on one strategy she learned to help her figure out a new word when she reads independently. She said, "I never knew I could make pictures in my head when I read! It's sort of like making my own video. So when I get to a word I don't know, I keep on reading and I look at the video in my head to see if I can figure out what makes sense." When students share such "Aha!" moments with each other, they demonstrate thoughtful reflection and make public their independent thinking.

Model Independence

Model a specific word-learning strategy by using a think-aloud to show students how you translate a strategy to your own independent use in the future. Share the following questions with students to model for them how to solve words independently:

- *How does the word start?*
- *Are there any chunks or parts I know?*
- *Is it like another word I know?*

- *What word makes sense here?*
- *What word looks right here?*
- *What word sounds right here?*

For instance, you could model for students how you analyze a multisyllabic word like *photosynthesis* by saying the following:

> *Many science terms have Greek or Latin roots, so it is important to be able to use the Divide and Conquer activity* (from Chapter 4) *independently to figure out a word's meaning. I know the prefix* photo *means "light," and the root* syn *means "with" or "together." I know the suffix* thes *means "put" or "place." So I can put them together, and I know that* photosynthesis *means "to put light with something." Now, if I meet the word* photojournalism *tomorrow, I can connect* photo, *which means "light" to the word* photograph, *and I can connect journalism to writing a news story. Then I can come up with the meaning of* photojournalism, *which is "a news story in photographs."*

Showing students how you analyze and decode multisyllabic and/or difficult words provides a window into your thinking and shows them how to be independent word learners.

Provide Guided Practice

Internalizing a strategy requires practice and opportunities to interact with others about the strategy (Graves, 2006). When students share with each other how they apply a word learning strategy, this talk can generate and reinforce learning. So, after you have modeled the strategy through thinking aloud, conference with individual students. Ask each student to find a page in a book and then think aloud to show you how he or she divides and conquers a new word independently.

Teaching in Action

The following conversation shows how Donna M. guided her third-grade students in collaborating to figure out the meaning of a new word:

Mrs. M: *Does anyone have a clue about what* revolution *means?*

Sakil: *Is it something like the word* moving?

Mrs. M: *OK, can anyone add anything to what Sakil said?*

Vicki: *It's what the door to a department store does. It goes around.*

Mrs. M: *You're both right.* Revolution *has to do with moving and going around. Did anyone try something different?*

Brenda: *It looks like* revolver. *But I don't think that fits here because this is science class!*

Mrs. M: *Great, Sakil, Vicki, and Brenda! Who can put all three clues together?*

Vicki: *Well, if* revolve *means "going around" and "moving,"* revolution *in science class might mean that something is going around something else.*

Mrs. M.: *Very good! You each connected something you knew with the word, and you are right, Vicki,* revolution *is an important word in our study of the solar system today.*

Donna's objective in asking "Does anyone have a clue . . ." is to encourage students to use their prior knowledge, share their ideas and take risks in word learning. Ultimately, Donna wants to help her students become independent in how they attack new words. She believes that this is the most important thing she can do to help them become successful, independent readers.

Prompts for Building Independence

To help students learn content-specific vocabulary, ELA words and testing vocabulary, I repeat an important quote from Chapter 4: "Words need to be pulled apart, put together, defined informally, practiced in speech, explained in writing, and played with regularly" (Kelley, Lesaux, Kieffer, & Faller, 2010; p. 13). To help students accomplish this, you can use simple prompts, like Donna's question, "Does anyone have a clue?" along with the prompts that follow.

Prompts for Learning New or Difficult Words

Use these two conversation starters with your students to help them become mindful of how they can independently access, learn, and use any new or difficult word:

- **"Tell me . . ."/"Tell us . . .":** This prompt directs students to explain how they decode new words. You can ask what connections or associations students may have made to other words they already know. You can also ask if the new word looks like another word

The Next Step in Vocabulary Instruction © 2012 by Karen Bromley, Scholastic Teaching Resources

that students know or if it contains a small word they know. Alternatively, you can ask students to share how they used context to figure out the new word. By beginning with "Tell me" or "Tell us," you honor the knowledge and word work students are capable of doing on their own. This conversation starter puts the responsibility for explaining in students' hands and replaces, or at least transfers, the power in the classroom from teacher to students.

- **"Notice . . .":** This prompt can direct students to remember to look for words in the classroom environment or a text they are reading and to use these words in their writing.

Teaching in Action

Brianna, a third-grade teacher, read Two Bad Ants *(1998) by Chris Van Allsburg to her class, and afterward students talked about choices, making decisions, and having adventures. Brianna used the story and discussion as a starter for a quick personal narrative writing task. She wrote three questions on chart paper and highlighted the three new words that she wanted students to use:*

1. *When did you make a good or bad* decision?

2. *What kind of* choice *did you have to make?*

3. *What* adventure *did you have as a result?*

Before students wrote, and during writing, Brianna circulated around the room reminding them, for example, to "Notice how adventure *is spelled on the chart and please spell it correctly in your narrative."*

Using a conversation starter like "Notice . . ." reminds students to find and use proper spelling for words as they write. It helps students become more resourceful as they find and use words on their own from classroom Word Walls, texts, personal journals and dictionaries, and so on. Like the conversation starter "Tell me," the "Notice" prompt helps students learn to access the information that is available to them as they become independent word learners.

Prompts for Teaching Content-Specific Vocabulary

Use the next two prompts for teaching content-specific vocabulary:

- **"Look for . . .":** Another simple way to direct students to use resources available to them is by using the conversation starter "Look for . . ." Teachers and students often overlook the visual clues available in print and electronic texts that give clues to key ideas, important words, and their meanings. Kelly and Clausen-Grace (2010) suggest doing a "text feature walk" with students. This involves alerting students to pay attention to the "table of contents, index, glossary, headings, bold words, sidebars, pictures and captions, and labeled diagrams" (p. 191).

  When you use "Look for," you remind students that key terms often appear in these text features and also in italics and/or in color. A good tip to share with students is that a short caption under a picture, illustration, or graphic often explains entire paragraphs of text succinctly. Additionally, chapter or selection overviews and summaries often contain the nuts-and-bolts vocabulary and concepts that are important for comprehension.

Together with the text features that usually contain key vocabulary, students can use context to infer word meanings and/or use the glossary, which is often an overlooked resource. Glossaries are easier to use than the dictionary since they contain far fewer words than dictionary definitions. The next prompt focuses specifically on these resources.

- **"Check your . . .":** directs students to use the resources they have to unlock difficult words, which may or may not appear in boldface or italics. The Common Core State Standards indicate that students should know how to use dictionaries, glossaries, and thesauruses (both print and digital). So, be sure your students understand the function of these materials and routinely use these references until they are comfortable using them independently. The glossaries and indexes found at the back of most content texts and many nonfiction books are a great help to students in determining the meanings and pronunciation of new words. And many classroom teachers have the resources to provide individual dictionaries to each student.

  Using these references can expand students' vocabularies, encourage their curiosity about words, and prompt their word consciousness. Be sure to have age-appropriate dictionaries for students to use. They may quickly be turned off if the dictionary is too large, has very small print, or if its definitions are too complex for them to comprehend.

  Age-appropriate dictionaries with pictures can be very helpful to struggling learners and ELLs as well. For older students, www.Kids.yahoo.com/reference is an online version of the American Heritage Dictionary. It includes definitions, pronunciations, etymologies, and links to encyclopedias and relevant articles. Wordsmyth (www.wordsmyth.net) provides definitions for children and older students along with synonyms, antonyms, and pronunciations.

These four prompts—"Tell me"/"Tell us," "Notice," "Look for," and "Check your"—put the responsibility for finding and learning new and difficult words in students' hands. Using these conversation starters allows you to be intentional, but not necessarily too direct, as you help students process and learn words. Students can gradually take the lead and become more independent in their own learning of all types of vocabulary.

Teach Content-Specific Vocabulary

Helping students read and make sense of words in conceptually dense content-area materials in science, math, and social studies is difficult work. These texts are packed with sophisticated, technical vocabulary and are often written at higher grade levels than many teachers realize. The following procedures and activities will help you ensure that students learn this important vocabulary and that they become independent learners, too.

- **Six Steps:** Try this procedure for teaching students the academic, content-specific Tier 3 vocabulary they need in order to be successful in school (Marzano & Pickering, 2005). It includes many of the things you have read about in this book. This example of direct instruction engages students in collaboration and the active use of new words they are learning:

  1. Provide an explanation or example of the word(s) (a picture or video image).
  2. Have students restate what they understand about the word(s).

The Next Step in Vocabulary Instruction © 2012 by Karen Bromley, Scholastic Teaching Resources

3. Have students draw a picture or a diagram in a notebook to remember the word(s).

4. Use activities that let students add information to the word(s) in the notebook.

5. Have students discuss the word(s) with each other.

6. Use games that require students to play with the word(s).

- **Vocabulary Notebook:** Figure 5.1 shows the Vocabulary Notebook entries of an eighth grader named Caytlyn, with definitions and drawings for the two Tier 3 words, *republic* and *empire.* These examples show the first three steps of Marzano and Pickering's procedure discussed above. Notice that Caytlyn includes the United States as an example of a *republic,* and she rates her understanding of the term as a "4." However, she does not include an example of *empire* and does not circle a number to indicate her level of understanding of *empire.* A quick look at Caytlyn's notebook prompted her teacher to ask her why she neglected to rate her understanding of *empire.* Caytlyn said, "I don't really know *empire* too well because I don't know the name of a country that is one." This helped her teacher see that he needed to follow up with a discussion of the meaning of the word *empire,* and a suitable example, to help Caytlyn really know the word well. By providing Caytlyn with an example of an empire of which she has prior knowledge, her teacher can provide crucial support to her understanding of the word. Do you see how a vocabulary notebook like this one might help you assess a student's vocabulary knowledge and understanding?

> ### Extend Your Thinking
>
> How are these steps different from ideas discussed in previous chapters? What do you believe are the most critical aspects of good vocabulary teaching? Why?

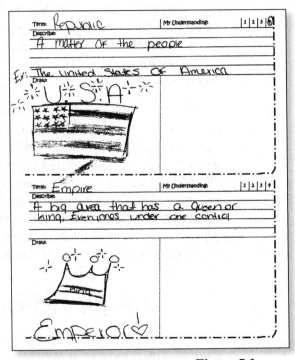

Figure 5.1

ACTIVITY ■ Alphaboxes

Materials: Alphaboxes template, pens or pencils

This activity (Hoyt, 1999) also helps students learn Tier 2 and Tier 3 words. Alphaboxes can be a prereading or postreading activity that promotes cooperative interactions among students. Alphaboxes can also be assigned as an individual activity to encourage independent vocabulary building.

After reading a book or content-area selection orally to students, display an Alphaboxes template that you've created (see sample in figure 5.2) and use it to talk about the important words heard in the story. Show students how to put several of these words in the correct boxes, for example, *migrate* in the M box. Each box should have only one entry, but as students become familiar with the activity, you can encourage them to add more than one key word to a box.

Encourage students to brainstorm words, ideas, and questions they have about the story.

They can also add short meanings for each of the words in a box. You may want to repeat this process a few times with different stories until students understand how to identify important ideas and vocabulary. Next, ask students to work in pairs or small groups. Give each group a copy of the book that was read and an Alphaboxes sheet. At first, ask for 5–8 words and, as students get the idea and begin to work effectively together, they can supply nearly all 24 boxes with important words and meanings.

Teaching in Action

One group of third graders who heard Jim Arnsoky's book All About Turtles *(Scholastic, 2000) came up with several words and definitions (see Figure 5.2). At the end of the activity, each group shared the words on its Alphaboxes sheet with the class. Lively discussions ensued as different groups shared different words for the same letters. At this point, groups can add words to blank boxes on their sheets, making it a vocabulary-stretching and comprehension-building activity.*

Alphaboxes			
A Arnosky (Jim): the author	B	C Carapace	D
E Eggs: what they lay	F	G	H Hatchling: a new turtle
I Insects: what they eat	J	K	L
M Migrate: they move	N	O Omnivorous: they eat meat & plants	P Plates: on their shell
Q	R	S Salt water: where tortoises live	T Tortoises: Turtles:
U	V	W	XYZ

Figure 5.2

This activity helps everyone review the big ideas and important terms in the story. Filling in the Alphaboxes prompts students to ask questions; make connections; explain, locate and identify unfamiliar words; and share different viewpoints. Supplying words allows students to contribute even if they remember a word but do not know its meaning, and vice versa. The activity promotes questioning (e.g., "What does *carapace* mean?") and rereading, talking, and further research to answer questions. By looking at a student's or group's completed Alphabox, you can tell which words and ideas students are unsure about, allowing you to return to a concept, reread parts of the story, discuss, and reteach a misconception.

ACTIVITY ■ **Alpha-picts**

Materials: 12-inch by 24-inch sheet of paper for each student, ruler, pencils, markers

Teaching in Action

This activity comes from Bob, an art teacher in an elementary school where the faculty has made vocabulary development an instructional focus. He had his third-grade students make Alpha-picts (see Figure 5.3). On 12- by 12-inch paper, students first used rulers to measure and draw 27 boxes. Next, they chose a word to write in each box and drew a picture for each word. Bob then displayed the students' Alpha-picts on a hall bulletin board for students, staff, and visitors to enjoy. Bob's vocabulary drawing activity shows one way that a creative art teacher can integrate literacy into an art class for students at all grade levels.

Figure 5.3 *An art teacher used Alpha-picts to build students' vocabularies.*

■ ■■ ■■■ ■ ■■■ ■■ ■■ ■■■ ■ ■■ ■■ ■■■ ■ ■■ ■■■ ■ ■■ ■■■ ■■ ■■ ■■■ ■ ■■■ ■

Extend Your Thinking

Read Vanessa Morrison and Lisa Wlodarczyk's idea for using Alphaboxes to help first-grade students identify target words after a read-aloud in "Revisiting read-aloud: Instructional strategies that encourage students' engagement with texts" in *The Reading Teacher* (2009), *63*(2), 110–118. Try their activity with a group of students. Be sure to model first for students how to fill in the boxes as the teacher did in the article.

ACTIVITY ■ 10 Important Words

Materials: 10 sticky notes for each group, pens or markers

This activity helps students learn to decide which words in a text are the most important (Yopp & Yopp, 2007). When students are able to find 10 important words in nonfiction, informational material, it means they have identified the major concepts or main ideas.

Begin the activity by putting students in groups of three or four with a range of abilities. Then give each group 10 sticky notes, have them read the text together, and put their notes near the 10 words they think are most important. As they read, students will move the notes around and identify different words as being more or less important. When everyone has finished, have students write each word on a sticky note. Then the entire class can make a tally of the most important words each group identified.

The 10 words that are identified most often are the "top 10" words from that text. You can engage students in a variety of writing, drawing, and acting-out activities using these words. You might give two or three of the words to each group and have them do something to demonstrate each word's meaning to the class. Here are some examples:

- Write two or three sentences to show what the word means.
- Dissect the word into parts and teach the class how to remember it.
- Act out the word.
- Create a drawing to show the word's meaning.
- Find two synonyms and two antonyms for the word.

ACTIVITY ■ Word Walls

Materials: Dragon Naturally Speaking software program (optional)

When you make the physical environment in your classroom rich with academic words, students can begin to become independent word learners and users. In Chapter 2, you read about the role of Word Walls in promoting vocabulary learning. It is worth mentioning again here how helpful these academic Word Walls are for struggling students and those learning English, because the terms in science, social studies, and math are especially difficult for these students.

Teaching in Action

Sean, a sixth-grade teacher, assigns English-speaking buddies to students newly arrived from Russia who do not speak English. The role of each buddy is to be a mentor and help his or her partner learn to pronounce the target content vocabulary. Sean's students also help their buddies who are acquiring English by using Dragon Naturally Speaking, a speech-to-print software program that eliminates the need for handwriting or keyboarding. With this program, which helps build oral skills first, students can say a word and the program converts it to print so students can see what the word looks like.

Most Word Walls are organized alphabetically, which helps students quickly access and use the words that appear on them. Since the alphabet provides a neatly structured and sequenced list of letters, it lends itself to other activities that build vocabulary. Here are some ideas for using ABC books to bolster vocabulary and build independence in word learning.

ACTIVITY ■ ABC Books

Materials: Alphaboxes template, markers, colored pencils, and material for collage art

Alphabet books have untapped potential for broadening students' content-specific vocabularies. ABC books allow you to differentiate instruction for struggling students and students with diverse needs. With this activity, you can engage students in productive, fun, independent word learning.

First, enlist the help of your library media specialist to find ABC books for your class. You will discover that there are ABC books written on every topic and in a range of difficulty levels. Next, flood your classroom with these books so students have a variety of models to read. Then share several different ABC books with students and point out the special features and formats of these books. Now, you are ready to have your students create their own ABC books. You can have students use an Alphaboxes template (see page 92) to list words and then have them use the writing process (plan, draft, revise, edit, and publish) to write a sentence for each letter and create a finished book.

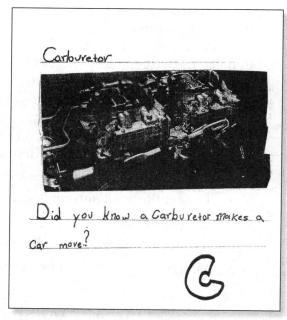

Figure 5.4 *ABC Books can take the form of questions.*

A combination of felt-tip markers, colored pencils, and collage art make interesting illustrations. Declan used a felt-tip marker and pictures cut from magazines to illustrate his *ABC Car Questions* book shown in Figure 5.4. Your school's art teacher can help your students with drawing their illustrations and choosing appropriate media and styles. Older students enjoy making ABC books for younger students or as a gift for a family member.

ACTIVITY ■ Two-Concept ABC Books

Materials: paper, crayons, sticky letters, markers, and other writing and drawing materials

To make the ABC book more challenging, have students create books that include two concepts.

Teaching in Action

In an after-school tutoring program, Kadieja, a struggling third grader, used an Alphabox and dictated words related to the topic of space to Ashley, her college student tutor. From a list of animals, Kadieja then circled one for each alphabet letter. Next, she wrote a sentence for each letter and made revisions, with Ashley's help, before making a final copy. In her book, Kadieja's ABC Book of Animals in Space, she used crayons, sticky letters, and felt-tip pens, as well as a picture of herself inserted into a space ship (see Figures 5.5 and 5.6).

ABC books are appropriate for building and reinforcing the vocabulary needed to understand science and social studies curriculum The following titles give you an idea of how ABC books might support your content instruction at a variety of grade levels:

- *Question & Answer ABCs of Weather*
- *The ABCs of Matter and Energy*
- *The ABCs of Fractions*
- *The ABCs of Africa*

- *The ABCs of Government*
- *The ABCs of Me*
- *The ABCs of Word Opposites*
- *The ABCs in Two Languages*

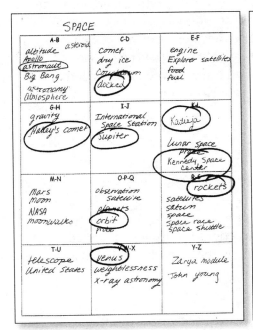

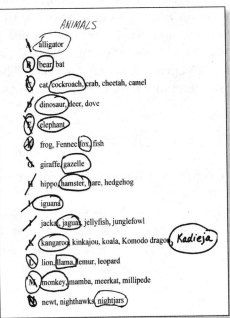

Figure 5.5 *Kadieja used two concepts—animals and space—for her ABC Book.*

Figure 5.6
Kadieja used collage, felt-tip markers, and a picture of herself to create her ABC Book.

ACTIVITY ▓ Science (ELA, Social Studies, or Math) Word Sorts

Since students can sort words in a number of different ways, word sorts are especially helpful to use in the content areas where academic vocabulary and meanings are often difficult to process and remember. Sorting words taps students' prior knowledge and reinforces their ability to see similarities and differences in the meaning and structure of words. Sorting words involves students in the active process of searching, comparing, contrasting, and analyzing words. Students learn to organize what they know about words and form generalizations they can apply to new words they see as they read (Bear, Invernizzi, Templeton, & Johnston, 2011).

I have found this strategy an engaging and effective way to help students at a variety of grade levels interact with one another to learn words. For example, to review important fourth-grade math vocabulary, I gave small groups of students the following words written on index cards to sort into logical categories; *denominator, multiplication, division, addition, subtraction, area, diameter, dimension, scalene, equilateral, median, isosceles, mode, perimeter, perpendicular, radius, range,* and *pyramid.* As students sorted the cards, they discussed the words and their meanings, struggled to make connections, and were challenged to then report to the class how and why they classified words the way they did. In the process of sharing, everyone learned how the terms and their relationships could be viewed differently. The word sort allowed for deeper processing and comprehension of vocabulary than might typically occur in reading the math text or by simply looking the words up in the dictionary and writing definitions.

Teach ELA Vocabulary

In the literature and/or basal readers of ELA reading, in the books you read to them, and in their daily lives, students are always encountering new words. Many of these Tier 2 words are not specific to a content area like science, math, or social studies, but they still may have elusive pronunciations and meanings. Remember, though, that you can modify many of the previous activities for teaching content-specific vocabulary to teach ELA and testing vocabulary. Here are some specific activities for building independence as students learn ELA words.

ACTIVITY ▓ Word Sort Stories

Materials: list of 12–15 words from reading selection for each group, scissors, index cards, markers, sticky notes (optional)

In this activity, students organize similar words from a book or a selection and use the words to tell a story and/or relate the main idea. (See Figure 5.8 for directions). This activity can be done by students working cooperatively together in groups, or it can be an individual activity to promote independence in word recognition and use.

Teaching in Action

A group of four fifth-grade students cut apart a sheet with vocabulary from Esperanza Rising *by Pam Muñoz Ryan (2002) (see Figure 5.7). This is a story about a young girl who moves from Mexico, where she is well off, to*

The Next Step in Vocabulary Instruction © 2012 by Karen Bromley, Scholastic Teaching Resources

California, where she is poor and must work as a farm laborer picking fruit and vegetables. Before reading the story, students sorted the words as shown in the second part of the figure. This gave them an opportunity to use their background knowledge and predict what might happen in the story. After students are part-way through a book or a content selection, they might resort the original words; they might even think of some new words they feel are important to the content and add these words to their sort.

Esperanza	rich	farming	vegetables	phoenix
poor	Valley Fever	Mexico	California	immigrants
Mama	strike	fruit	Mexican labor camp	servant

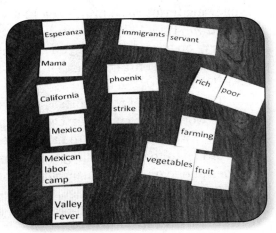

Figure 5.7 *Sorting words before reading prepares students for* Esperanza Rising *by Pam Muñoz Ryan.*

DIRECTIONS FOR WORD SORT STORIES

Purpose/Description: As a prereading word-sort strategy, this taps prior knowledge and builds vocabulary. As a postreading strategy, it reinforces vocabulary and comprehension. It involves organizing and using key terms from a book or selection to tell a story and/or relate the main idea.

You Need: Choose 12–15 key words from a book or a content-area selection and type them into a table. Make a copy for each group, and have a pair of scissors for each group.

1. Give each group a copy of words to cut up.
2. Tell students to sort the words first into categories.
3. Have students use the words to make an outline for how they think the story/selection goes together.
4. Ask each group of students to tell a story from the word sort and share the ideas they developed. Have them explain why they organized words the way they did.

Variations:
- Give each group a few blank cards and have students add key terms they need to create their story.
- Use the word sorts as a prewriting prompt for writing a summary of the story/selection.
- As students read the selection, have them identify key terms on sticky notes and use these for the activity.

Figure 5.8

ACTIVITY ■ Story Grammar Word Sort

Materials: 3-inch by 5-inch index cards, marker

You can also use a word sort to teach and reinforce ELA vocabulary. For example, choose several key words from a book or story (and print them on index cards) that relate to the following terms (also printed on index cards): *characters, setting, theme, plot, problem, solution.* Then have students sort words into the categories and share their sorts with the class. Or, try "open sorts" where you supply several words from the story or book written on cards and then have students sort them in any way that makes sense to them before sharing their reasons for the sort with the class.

The purpose of word sorts is to have students examine words printed on cards and put these words in groups or categories according to how the words seem to go together. Students can sort words according to meaning or conceptually related terms. Or, they can sort words according to form or spelling similarities; for example, initial and/or final consonants, blends, rimes/phonograms, singular, plural, prefixes, suffixes, roots, capital or lowercase letters, and so on. When students can articulate the reason for their sort and pronounce each word, the activity promotes not only word identification but also inferential and creative thinking.

ACTIVITY ■ Word Solver

Materials: lanyard, card, marker

Each week, appoint a different student who knows many Tier 2 and Tier 3 words to be the classroom Word Solver, Word Expert, or Word Helper. This student can help you during reading and/or writing workshop, when you are providing direct instruction to one group and the rest of the class is reading self-selected material, by being the "go-to" person when someone is stuck on a word. Or, appoint this student to help others during independent reading and/or writing time. The Word Solver should have a large reading and writing vocabulary and a good handle on analyzing difficult words. He or she should be able to help peers use context, word parts, and associations with prior knowledge to unlock difficult vocabulary. Give the student a lanyard to wear with a card attached that identifies his or her role (see Figure 5.9). Acting as a Word Solver builds that student's confidence and independence as a word learner as he or she helps peers who need assistance.

When students are responsible for helping peers read and write new and/or hard words, they quickly become independent themselves.

Figure 5.9 *Each day, let a different student be the Word Solver or Word Expert to help classmates.*

Teaching in Action

April chose three of her fourth graders to wear lanyards identifying each as a Word Solver. Before she announced the names of these students to the class, April reviewed with them how to use the glossary at the back of their science and social studies books (and many nonfiction titles where definitions and pronunciations of difficult words appear). April rotates the helpers weekly and finds that students clamor to wear a lanyard and be a Word Solver. April says, "They seem to be more aware of how to figure out hard words, and I see pride on the faces of the Word Solvers who now have new status in the classroom."

ACTIVITY ■ "Key" Word Strategy

Materials: chart paper, marker, "Key" Words Summary reproducible (page 140)

Use this activity after students have read or listened to a selection or story to help them identify key words and then write a summary. First, help students identify three important words that represent the big ideas in the story. Then guide them as they create a summary statement or report, which you can transcribe for them. ELLs and students with language difficulties can draw a picture for each word and an illustration for the sentence.

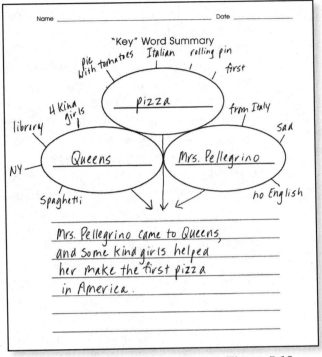

Figure 5.10

Teaching in Action

Bev used the "Key" Word Strategy with her second-grade class after reading them the story How Pizza Came to Queens *by Dayal Khalsa (1989). Here are the steps she took (and posted on chart paper):*

1. *Read or listen to a story.*

2. *Choose three "big" main idea words. Write each in one of the ovals on the "Key" Word Summary reproducible.*

3. *Add words that support each main idea word. If there are no supporting words, change your main idea word.*

4. *On the lines, write a sentence that uses all three words.*

Bev's students identified the following three terms: pizza, Queens, *and* Mrs. Pellegrino. *Then they added detail words, like* pie with tomatoes, Italian, rolling pin, *and so on for* pizza *(see Figure 5.10). Finally, they dictated a summary sentence using each of the words that they felt held the main idea of the story.*

To build vocabulary knowledge, have students work in pairs and then in small groups to share main idea words and why they chose them. Then make a list of all the main idea words the pairs or groups identified and discuss each word and the personal meanings that emerge. This builds awareness of different perspectives and interpretations. You can also have students revise their main idea sentences by adding one or more supporting details, adjectives, and adverbs.

Using graphic organizers like "Key" Word Summary and "Magnet" Words (see pages 140, 141), encourages students to discover what is most important in a story or selection and requires them to support their opinions.

ACTIVITY ■ **Zooming In/Zooming Out**

Materials: Zooming In and Zooming Out reproducible (page 142), pens

The graphic organizer in this activity can be used to build content-specific vocabulary and/or ELA vocabulary. "Zooming In" provides a close examination, or "microscopic look," at a word or concept, and "Zooming Out" gives a "panoramic view" of it (see Figure 5.11). Thus, the microscopic look is a rectangle, and the panoramic view is a circle that is viewed from a telescope. It can be used before, during, or after hearing or reading a story or selection (Bromley, 2002; Harmon & Hedrick, 2000), and it blends word learning with concept development for students in grades 4–8. When you use the strategy before reading, you can activate and record students' prior knowledge. When you use it during reading, you develop comprehension as students rely on context for word meanings. When you use it after reading, you support students' interactions with text as they review and reread together to find information.

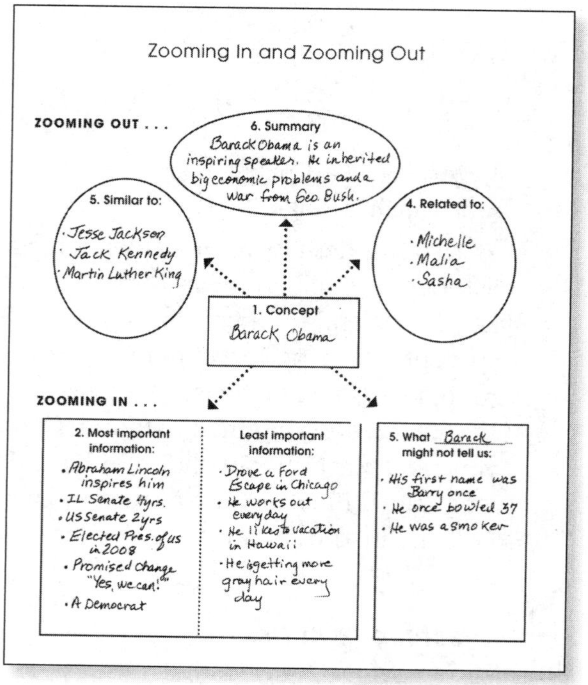

Creating this organizer can be a powerful experience. Your students will share ideas and use critical thinking to arrive at "close-up" views (most and least important information related to the word) and "big picture" views (similarities and relationships to the word) of the world. They brainstorm, read, and discuss text to form a summary statement. But, as with any graphic organizer, use this one sparingly, perhaps for one or two of the most critical concepts in a unit or text. Overuse of any graphic organizer isn't helpful for students, so vary the way you assist them in looking closely at a text and considering its broader implications. Then post completed organizers for students to refer to in class discussions and writing.

Figure 5.11

ACTIVITY ■ **Vo-back-ulary**

Materials: chart paper, marker, 5-inch by 8-inch index cards

You can use this activity to reinforce ELA words as well as content-specific words. It actively involves students in recognizing words, providing clues, guessing, and turn-taking.

Teaching in Action

Kristen, a special education teacher, finds Vo-back-ulary (Bromley, 2002) especially popular with her middle school students because they work together to identify a target word. Kristen uses Vo-back-ulary to review and reinforce science and social studies words that are particularly difficult for her students. But you might just as easily use it to reinforce ELA or testing vocabulary. Kristen lists the target words on the board or chart paper and prints each one on an index card. She pronounces each word and has students repeat the word and review its

The Next Step in Vocabulary Instruction © 2012 by Karen Bromley, Scholastic Teaching Resources

meaning. Then she tapes an index card to a student's back without revealing what the word is. The student then strolls around the room so the class can see the word printed on the card. Next, the class gives the student clues to the unknown word, and the student guesses until he or she is correct and chooses someone to go next.

Tell students that to begin, it is a good idea to model clues that deal with meaning (see the clues below for *penguin*):

- *"It lives where it's cold."*
- *"It is black and white."*
- *"It has a beak."*

Offer easier clues related to structure last:

- *"It has five letters."*
- *"It starts with a p."*

Vo-back-ulary is active. It focuses on word meanings and requires students to take turns and use their schema. Students must think about a word's meaning and how to help someone figure it out. Kristen says, "My students have a lot of fun with Vo-back-ulary and beg to play it every day. They remember the words because they connect their own personal meanings to them."

Teach Testing Vocabulary

Words found in test directions, such as *passage, sentence, topic, article, underline, circle,* and *compare,* comprise their own critical area of school vocabulary. If students cannot understand the vocabulary in test directions, their chances of doing well on that test are greatly diminished.

ACTIVITY ▦ Q & A (Question & Answer)

Materials: chart paper, marker, sticky notes

Teaching in Action

Laurie and the other fourth-grade teachers on her team examined the directions on their state's ELA test. They identified several words they believed were worth teaching and reinforcing with students. Then Laurie had her class play the Q & A game below to gain familiarity with this important vocabulary.

First, Laurie prints these words on a large chart in a table format (see Figure 5.12). Next, she focuses her class's attention on each word. She pronounces each word once, exaggerates each syllable

"Directions" Vocabulary		
passage	sentence	topic
article	questions	predict
problem	detail	section
heading	information	phrase
author	paragraph	newspaper
dictionary	according to	mostly
context	describes	mistakes
correction	punctuation	grammar
usage	compare	complete
different	opinion	contrast

Figure 5.12

on a second repetition, then has the class say each word chorally with her. Finally, she asks individual students to explain or define each word. Then Laurie covers each word with a sticky note and has a student pull one sticky note away to reveal a word labeled "Answer." The student then poses a question that matches that answer.

Laurie models the first question for students by asking a question for which the answer is the exposed word. For example, if the word is *mistakes*, the question might be, "What is the opposite of correct answers?" At the conclusion of the game, when all of the words are exposed, the class pronounces all the words in unison.

Laurie and her colleagues believe this valuable preparation helps students be more successful in answering test questions. Laurie says, "I feel this activity builds awareness of important testing terms and gives students practice with them so they can approach test-taking with confidence."

You can also build your students' knowledge of testing vocabulary with other activities in this chapter. Don't overlook activities like Vocabulary Notebooks, ABC Books, Vo-back-ulary, and others. Using testing terms in place of content-specific words and ELA words in these activities also works well to teach and reinforce the terms.

Daily Calendar: Words, Words, Words

Use the 30 activities in this Daily Calendar: Words, Words, Words to provide opportunities for independent word learning on the Internet. The activities involve students in using the Web to learn more about digital literacy and add related new words and meanings to their lexicons. After completing this month's calendar of activities, students can proudly call themselves a *wired word sleuth* or a *private verbal investigator*. The calendar can also be sent home for parents to use with students and their siblings. If there is no Internet access at home, the public library has computers where students and families can do the activities in this list.

DAILY CALENDAR: WORDS, WORDS, WORDS

Week 1: Getting Started

1. **Learn how** to be safe on the Internet at www.SafetyClicks.com, where you can play a game to build your Internet savvy, visit sites for kids, see a cartoon, and get tips on using the Web.

2. **Ask your teacher** if you can share the important ideas from Safety Clicks with the class. Teach classmates the terms you learned, for example, *BOT, instant messenger, password, offline, Kids Only,* and *online.*

3. **Interview your school's library media specialist** or computer teacher to find out what an Internet filtering program is, what it does, and if your school uses one. Ask about why it is required in most schools in the United States.

4. **Go to** this site: http://school.aol.com and click on "Take a Virtual Trip" to find out what *virtual trip* means. Also at this site, find out what an archive is and why you might use one.

5. **Find out how** to be polite on the Web and learn the basics of surfing the Net at www.albion.com/ netiquette/corerules.html. After reading the information here, you should be able to define *netiquette, online behavior,* and *cyberspace.* Share your new words with a friend.

 The Next Step in Vocabulary Instruction © 2012 by Karen Bromley, Scholastic Teaching Resources

Week 2: Safe Search Engines

6. **With your parents** and a sister or brother, visit www.yahooligans.com/parents. Find out what the term *safe surfing* means and how to practice it. What is a privacy policy? Ask your teacher if you can share these terms with your classmates, library media specialist, and computer teacher.

7. **Visit the powerful kids' search engine** at http://kids.yahooligans.com. Think of a word for a topic you are learning about in school and type it into the search box. What new information did you learn? What questions do you still have? Click on "Ask Earl" and see if he can answer your question.

8. **Visit the CyberSleuth Kids search engine** (cybersleuth-kids.com) and click on "classroom clipart." Notice all the categories of pictures there are at this site. How many different pictures can you download from music? dinosaurs? transportation?

9. **Go to KidsClick** at http://sunsite.berkeley.edu/kidsclick!. Choose a word from one of the 600 subjects this search engine offers and do a search on that word. What did you learn? Pick two more subject words and do a search on them to see what you can learn.

10. **Make a guess** about what the word *database* means. Before you guess, think about what you just learned as you visited the last three search engine sites. Check your guess against your classroom dictionary or find the definition of this word at http://merriam-webster.com.

11. **In the database** at kidsnook.com, check out the multisensory e-flashcards that KidsNook offers. These flashcards teach vocabulary by giving you a moving picture to connect to each printed term. What three new terms did you learn?

12. **Look closely** at the e-flashcards at KidsNook. How do these flashcards help young children learn words easily? What three things may be the answer?

Week 3: Puzzles & Games

13. **Learn new slang** and technical vocabulary at www.randomhouse.com/words. Find answers to your questions about words, get suggestions for new words to learn, and play a variety of vocabulary games.

14. **Find clip art** and tools at puzzlemaker.com. Make up your own puzzles in different styles using vocabulary words from your own reading and writing. Share the puzzles with your teacher and a friend.

15. **Find definitions** and information about many words and subjects at encyclopedia.com. Also find information on important events in world history that happened on this day and connect to a "reference desk" with links to dictionaries, almanacs, and thesauruses.

16. **Find a directory** of games at www.surfnetkids.com/games. They are listed by type (such as crossword or jigsaw) and topic (such as science or history), and there's also a search function for specific games.

17. **Ask a friend** to play a science or social studies game with you at the Web site above. What did you learn as you played the game together?

18. **Contact "real world experts"** at www.askanexpert.com who can answer questions about specific subjects as they help you learn the meanings of new words.

19. **Try your luck** at a new "Word Game of the Day" at www.m-w.com/game where you can try different puzzle formats, like "Transform Brainstorm," which lets you change a word into another word, one letter at a time, using clues to the word's meaning.

Week 4: More Puzzles & Games

20. **Create a story** at www.eduplace.com/tales using 10–15 of your own words like a plural noun, a large number, an adjective, and so on. At this site, you can publish the "Wacky Web Tales" you create and read the tales other students have written.

21. **Learn geography** at www.maps.com, where you can see all kinds of different maps and play geography games that teach and test your knowledge of place names around the world.

22. **On a map** of the United States, locate the place where you live. What states border your state? Locate the capital of your state and locate Washington, D.C., our country's capital. How far are you from each city?

23. **Click on** your grade level at Ben's Guide for U.S. Government for Kids at http://bensguide.gpo.gov to learn about all aspects of our government. Find many things including what the symbols of the U.S. government are, how laws are made, the election process, and a lot of games and other government Web sites for kids.

24. **Learn a new word** based on a weekly theme each day at www.wordsmith.org/awad/index.html, with its definition, pronunciation, history, usage, and a quotation using the word. You can subscribe and receive it automatically.

25. **Learn about animals** at www.zoobooks.com, where you will find games and artwork by other students and lots of other fun activities to help you expand your vocabulary power. Name one new animal you had never heard of and learned about.

26. **Find pictures** of things and their definitions in different languages at www.pdictionary.com. Play the games you find here, and if you like them, follow the directions and share this site with a friend.

Week 5: Finishing Up

27. **Earn a diploma** from "Vocabulary University" at www.vocabulary.com, where you can do all kinds of different puzzles and games that build your vocabulary. Show your teacher and parents this Web site.

28. **Make a list** of at least ten new words or concepts you have learned this month. Share this list with your teacher and parents. Look the words up at www.merriamwebster.com and be sure to tell these people what each word means.

29. **Review** what you have learned about using the Internet and computer this month. Go back to www. SafetyClicks.com, where you first played a game to build your Internet savvy. Thinking about what you have learned, what three questions would you add to the test at this site?

30. **CONGRATULATIONS!** After completing this month's calendar of activities, you can proudly call yourself a *wired word sleuth* or a *private verbal investigator*. What do you think these terms mean?! Share these terms and their meanings with your teacher and classmates.

CHAPTER 6

Playing With Words

"What did the alien say to the book? 'Take me to your reader!'"

—Joseph,
six years old

Six-year-old Joseph proudly tells his mother this joke and begins to giggle before he can even say the final line. This type of humor, which relies on wordplay (*reader* substituted for *leader*), appeals to young children. As well as being lighthearted and fun, jokes and humor using wordplay can have a huge role in developing students' vocabulary. Books full of jokes and wordplay can introduce new vocabulary and develop multiple meanings as they bring laughter and a feeling of community to your classroom.

According to the Common Core State Standards for ELA (2011), students should be able to "demonstrate understanding of figurative language, word relationships, and nuances in word meanings." This chapter provides strategies to help your students develop this knowledge and enjoy the playful aspects of language as they gain a greater awareness and appreciation of words.

Let's briefly review in this last chapter some things you've read about in previous chapters. What does good vocabulary teaching look like? The effective vocabulary teacher exhibits word consciousness with students and shares his or her excitement about language as well as the benefits of learning words. An effective vocabulary teacher adheres to several guidelines for effective vocabulary instruction. These following key principles discussed in Chapter 3 are the basis for the strategies and activities you have been reading about in this book:

- Select words and assess word knowledge.
- Teach a few words directly and deeply.
- Determine when to teach new words.
- Activate students' schema and build metacognition.
- Teach students to use context.
- Examine word structure.

- Teach for independence.
- Provide guided practice.

What is missing from this list? Fun and playfulness! Vocabulary can grow exponentially when you give students opportunities to have fun with language and experiment with words.

Appreciating Humor

Knowing how humor develops across grade levels can guide you in the kinds of wordplay activities you use with your students. Children of different ages begin to understand and appreciate different kinds of humor at different stages in their development as shown in Figure 6.1. But students vary in their individual growth, development, and appreciation of humor, so this sequence is only a guide. The joke that introduced this chapter appealed to a 6-year-old, but younger and older students might also find it funny. Different kinds of humor can be appreciated by students of many ages.

DEVELOPMENT OF HUMOR	
Approximate Ages	**Type of Humor and Examples**
Ages 6–8	Conceptual mismatches (*reader* for *leader; cup* for *hat; banana* for *telephone*)
Ages 7–11	Multiple meanings and ambiguity (*A cow scrubbing its back with a brush* [a toothbrush] *while singing and taking a bath in a bathtub.*)
Ages 10–12	Irony, satire, and sarcasm (*He is as smart as a soap dish.*)

Adapted from McGhee, 1984; Pexman, Glenwright, Krol, & James, 2005

Figure 6.1 *Children's appreciation of different kinds of humor develops at different ages.*

Ways to Play With Words

Authors often play with words by creating a mismatch between or among concepts. In the joke that began this chapter, for example, the word *reader* is substituted for *leader*. Authors also use words that have multiple meanings and are ambiguous. *A cow scratching its back with a brush* (a toothbrush) *while taking a bath in a bathtub.* And, authors use irony, satire, and sarcasm; for example: *He is as smart as a soap dish.* Authors use a variety of wordplay tools to achieve this kind of lighthearted, lively language that appeals to students and adults (see Figure 6.2 on the next page). If you use any of these wordplay tools, be sure to provide students with the accompanying examples but also share examples from stories, books, and poems that are authentic uses of wordplay in context.

Extend Your Thinking

Look at the list of wordplay tools in Figure 6.2 on the next page. Which language tools would students between the ages of 6–8, 7–11, and 10–12 most likely understand and enjoy? Which would be easiest for them to write after you have shared examples?

The Next Step in Vocabulary Instruction © 2012 by Karen Bromley, Scholastic Teaching Resources

WAYS TO PLAY WITH WORDS

Acronym	Use of letters to represent words	Example: SCUBA, SNAFU, AWOL
Acrostic	Use of each letter of a name or a word to begin other descriptive words	Example: K—knitter, A—artistic , R—runner, E—early-bird, N—near-sighted (KAREN)
Alliteration	Repeating the same sound at the beginning of two or more words	Example: *soggy, soupy, slimy weather*
Homographs	Words that are spelled the same but have different meanings	Examples: *hand* (noun and verb), *ball* (noun and verb), *jam* (noun and verb) The little finger on my left *hand* hurts. I asked students to *hand* in their papers. He threw the *ball* and broke the window. When he hit her, she began to *ball*. I love your homemade strawberry *jam*. He tried to *jam* the screwdriver into the opening.
Homophones	Words that sound alike but have different spellings and meanings	Examples: *steel, steal; sea, see*
Hyperbole	An exaggeration used to express an idea or opinion	Example: *The mouse looked as big as an elephant.*
Idiom	A figurative phrase that is not meant literally	Example: *My mom had a frog in her throat.*
Irony	Says one thing but has a second, usually opposite meaning	Example: *We were overwhelmed by the gift of one penny.*
Metaphor	Comparing different things to show their likeness	Example: *The sun was a giant egg yolk in the sky.*
Onomatopoeia	Words that imitate real sounds	Example: *Pow!, Wham!, Zap!, Zing!*
Personification	Giving human qualities to animals or inanimate objects	Example: *The pencil leapt from my fingers.*
Simile	Comparing two different things using the word *like* or *as*	Example: *Her teeth were as white as pearls.*
Synonyms	Words that mean the same thing (or nearly the same thing)	Example: *wet, soggy, moist*

Figure 6.2 *Alert students to these wordplay tools as you meet them during read-alouds.*

Wordplay Activities

There are many ways to encourage students to use wordplay as a means of improving their vocabulary knowledge. Below are several ideas for direct instruction, guided practice, and independence that I suggest you adapt to fit your students and curriculum.

Teach Words Directly

ACTIVITY ■ Wordplay and Poetry Books

Materials: a variety of wordplay and poetry books (see below)

One of the easiest ways to build students' appreciation of wordplay is by reading books to them that include wordplay and poetry (see pp. 109 and 110). These books often feature language and language patterns that are unique and humorous. Reading them with your students and making them available in the classroom are good ways to enjoy language together and show students how words work. So flood your classroom with riddle books, joke books, poetry books, alphabet books, rhymes, and just-for-fun stories.

Remember that poetry and many wordplay books are best shared orally so that the sounds and the rhythm of language can be fully appreciated. So keep this literature close at hand, and when you have a few minutes, read wordplay books and short, humorous poems to your class. This is a good way to sensitize students to the rhyme, rhythm, cadence, and visual pictures that words can create. Students need to hear, read, see, and understand the wordplay tools authors use before you can expect them to engage in their own written wordplay.

ACTIVITY ■ Writing Poetry

Materials: a variety of poetry collections, dictionaries and thesauruses, pens or pencils

Poetry is popular with students of all ages because of its brevity and rhythm. Poet Paul Janeczko (1999) says, "Writing poetry gives you a chance to fall in love with language again and again." It is also another way to play with words and, in the process, develop your students' vocabularies. Poets write with vivid and concrete language, often describing what they see, hear, and feel. So, read poems first to students and then set the stage for writing by engaging their senses—seeing, hearing, touching, feeling, listening, and tasting.

Vocabulary, an important aspect of good writing, also contributes to listening comprehension, reading comprehension, and fluency. Zarry (1999) found that students who received vocabulary instruction that engaged them in playful activities used the words they learned more often in their writing and wrote narratives of a higher quality than students who did not receive this instruction. The students who learned and used more words each received a thesaurus and were encouraged to select their own words to use in their writing and create their own definitions and sentences for each word. So, supply your students with a dictionary and/or thesaurus and watch what happens when you encourage them to use these resources.

The Next Step in Vocabulary Instruction © 2012 by Karen Bromley, Scholastic Teaching Resources

WORDPLAY BOOKS

- *WordPlay Cafe: Cool Codes, Priceless Punzles & Phantastic Phonetec Phun* (Williamson Kids Can! Series) by Michael Kline (Ideals Children's Books, 2005). (Grades 3–8). This book builds vocabulary in a variety of ways. It includes "Pundits," a combination of art and word games that encourages both visual and auditory learners.

- *Wordplay: Fun Games for Building Reading and Writing Skills in Children With Learning Difficulties* by Lori Goodman (McGraw-Hill, 2004). (All ages). These playful, multisensory, easy-to-use games build reading and writing skills including learning the alphabet, phonics, rhyming, parts of speech, and comprehension.

- *Top Secret: A Handbook of Codes, Ciphers, and Secret Writing* by Paul Janeczko (Candlewick, 2006). (Grades 4–8). This guide to secret writing includes the origin and reasons for different codes with historical examples. It contains information and exercises (with answers) on deciphering codes and gives students the tools to make their own field kit. It also features codes and ciphers, invisible ink recipes, and a number of concealment techniques.

- *Scien-Trickery: Riddles in Science* by Patrick Lewis (Harcourt, 2004). (Grades 1–6). Rhymes describe something related to science that readers can guess from the clues; the answers appear upside down at the bottom of each page. Topics include the Galápagos Islands, laser beams, germs, Albert Einstein, magnets, oxygen, gravity, electricity, planets, maps, humidity, numbers, constellations, decibels, oceans, dinosaurs, properties of rust, and the moon.

- *Rhyme & PUNishment: Adventures in Wordplay* by Brian Cleary (Millbrook Press, 2006). (Grades 3–7). This collection of silly and sophisticated puns uncovers double meanings that are kind dove hiding in everyday phrases. A helpful pun-unciation guide is included on porpoise to help ewe understand pronunciation.

- *Doodle Dandies: Poems That Take Shape* by J. Patrick Lewis (Atheneum, 1998). (Grades 2–6). This is a book of "concrete poetry," meaning there is a poem on every page written in the shape of the object the poem describes.

- *Walking the Bridge of Your Nose: Wordplay Poems Rhymes* by Michael Rosen (Kingfisher, 1995). (Grades 1–6). This anthology of lighthearted poems, riddles, tongue twisters, parodies and puns can be read and enjoyed many times.

- *Fire Words: A Book of Wordplay Poems* by John Foster (Oxford Children, 2000). (Grades K–3). This collection includes rhymes and chants, tongue twisters and limericks, riddles and puns, and also shape poems, surprising spellings, and puzzling punctuation.

- *Max's Dragon* by Kate Banks (Farrar, Straus & Giroux, 2008). (Grades 1–3). Unexpected things happen while Max plays with his invisible dragon. The story includes many rhyming-word combinations, such as found-ground, faster-disaster, sneeze-breeze, and furry-worry.

- *Max's Words* by Kate Banks (Farrar, Straus & Giroux, 2006). (Grades 2–5). Max cuts random words out of newspapers and magazines and arranges them into a story that he tells his brothers. This book teaches students about words, sentences, and storytelling.

- *The Boy Who Loved Words* by Roni Schotter (Schwartz & Wade, 2006). (Grades 2–5). A boy nicknamed Wordsworth uses creative and unusual words like *tintinnabulating* to describe his thoughts, feelings, and actions. A glossary gives meanings for the often strange and interesting words that Wordsworth loves to use.

- *Some Smug Slug* by Pamela Edwards (HarperTrophy, 1996) (Grades 2–5) Alliteration and multisyllabic words tell the story of a slug that does not listen well, "A self-assured slug slinks up the side of a suspicious sloping surface. Scoffing at shouts of 'Stop' from spectators, the smug slug finally reaches the summit."

- *Clara Caterpillar* by Pamela Edwards (HarperCollins, 2001). (Grades 2–5). This book is filled with alliterative and multisyllabic prose, for example, "By camouflaging herself, Clara Caterpillar, who becomes a cream-colored butterfly, courageously saves Catisha, the crimson colored butterfly from a hungry crow."

POETRY BOOKS

- *A Child's Introduction to Poetry: Listen While You Learn About the Magic Words That Have Moved Mountains, Won Battles, and Made Us Laugh and Cry* by Michael Driscoll (Black Dog & Leventhal, 2003). (Grades 1–6).

- *Big Talk: Poems for Four Voices* by Paul Fleischman (Candlewick, 2008). (Grades 3–8). The three poems in this book contain lines to be read aloud in unison by four voices. Reading them motivates students to pay attention to each other and the "beat" of the poem.

- *Joyful Noise: Poems for Two Voices* by Paul Fleischman (HarperCollins, 2004). (Grades 3–8). This book's humorous, fact-filled poems about insects are meant to be read aloud by two people.

- *I Am Phoenix: Poems for Two Voices* by Paul Fleischman (HarperCollins, 1989). (Grades 3–8). The humorous, fact-filled poems about birds in this collection are meant to be read aloud by two people.

- *The Random House Book of Poetry for Children* by Jack Prelutsky (Random House, 1983). (Grades 1–8). An anthology of 572 poems that covers the best children's poetry up to the '80s, from Mother Goose to Lewis Carroll, written for students of all ages.

- *A Light in the Attic* by Shel Silverstein (HarperCollins, 2001). (Grades 1–8). This collection contains short, light-hearted poetry accompanied by simple black-and-white drawings that delight the senses and bring a smile.

- *Hip Hop Speaks to Children: A Celebration of Poetry With a Beat* by Nikki Giovanni (Sourcebooks Jabberwocky, 2008). (Grades 2–6). Giovanni, a celebrated poet, has compiled poetry with a beat, read by many of the original authors including Maya Angelou, Langston Hughes, Eloise Greenfield, and Mos Def. The collection also includes a CD.

- *Hey, You!: Poems to Skyscrapers, Mosquitoes, and Other Fun Things* by Paul Janeczko (HarperCollins, 2007). (Grades 2–6). This is a diverse collection of poems written on myriad topics.

- *A Foot in the Mouth: Poems to Speak, Sing, and Shout* by Paul Janeczko (Candlewick, 2009). (Grades 2–6). A collection of fun, lighthearted poems that students will enjoy having read to them.

- *Reading Poetry in the Middle Grades: 20 Poems and Activities That Meet the Common Core Standards and Cultivate a Passion for Poetry* by Paul Janeczko (Heinemann, 2011). (Grades 2–8). Includes 20 different poems, both contemporary and classic, that show how to use poetry as a vehicle for teaching metaphor, literary criticism, writing, and more.

- *Love That Dog* by Sharon Creech (Scholastic, 2003). (Grades 3–8). Miss Stretchberry nudges her student Jack to write free verse poetry in his journal about poems by Walter Dean Myers which relate to Jack's life.

- *Hate That Cat* by Sharon Creech (HarperCollins, 2010). (Grades 3–8). In this sequel to *Love That Dog*, Jack learns about onomatopoeia and synonyms as he continues to write free verse poetry about famous poems and the cats in his own life, a fat black one in particular.

- *Wham! It's a Poetry Jam* by Sara Holbrook (Boyds Mills Press, 2002). (Grades 2–8). This is a guide to performing poetry alone and in groups with suggestions for setting up poetry performance contests.

- *If I Were in Charge of the World and Other Worries* by Judith Viorst (Macmillan, 1981). (Grades 1–4). A collection of poems on everyday topics that young students will enjoy.

- *All the Small Poems and Fourteen More* by Valerie Worth (Farrar, Straus & Giroux, 1994). (Grades 1–4). Lighthearted poems about porches, frogs, chairs, daisies, pebbles, and more, illustrated by Natalie Babbitt.

- *Knock at a Star: A Child's Introduction to Poetry* by X. J. Kennedy and Dorothy M. Kennedy (Little, Brown, 1999). (Grades 3–8). A collection of poems arranged in categories, including poems that make you smile, poems that send messages, share feelings, or have a repeating beat, as well as limericks, song lyrics, and haikus.

When writing poetry, it is a good idea to have students brainstorm their topic first and list all the possible words they might use. From the list of words they generate, have students choose the best words to describe what they want to say—words that convey as precisely as possible the image or feeling they want to communicate. Brainstorming as a prewriting step does several things:

- Stretches students' vocabulary and word knowledge
- Encourages searching for the "sizzle" or "sparkle" words that say exactly what a student wants to say
- Sensitizes students to the nuances of word meanings
- Leads to better writing because students are more likely to use precise, vivid language

Another way to nudge students to think of words that "sizzle" or "sparkle" is to give them sentences with less-than-perfect word choices and have them come up with better alternatives. Here are some examples (Bromley, 2002):

Precise nouns:

1. She faced <u>a lot of hard things</u> bravely. (*problems, obstacles*)
2. I've come to <u>the general idea</u> that golf can be fun. (*conclude, see*)
3. He found <u>little pieces</u> of glass all over the floor. (*shards, bits*)

Strong verbs:

1. She <u>looked very closely at</u> the bird. (*examined, studied*)
2. The woman <u>called very loudly</u>. (*screamed, yelled*)
3. The child <u>looked angrily</u> at her mother. (*glared, stared*)

Similes:

1. as loud as a_____ (*sonic boom, bomb exploding*)
2. as slow as (a) _____ (*tortoise, molasses*)
3. as fresh as a_____ (*daisy, $100 bill*)

In the following example, a sixth grader used descriptive words to capture the speed and direction of a stream. This was the *V* page in an alphabet book of poetry his class wrote as part of a science unit on water:

> "Once there was a stream *violently veering* like a snake swerving and slithering to catch its next *victim* or *vanquish* an enemy making small *vortexes* as it moved across a *vast* stretch of land."

Extend Your Thinking

What other wordplay tools found in Figure 6.2 did this student use?

- *Writing Acrostics:* The acrostic poem is one of many types of simple poems that can help propel students to use wordplay tools and find just-right vocabulary (see Figure 6.3). Writing informational acrostic poetry after reading and researching in content areas provides a creative way for students to use key vocabulary and factual details (Frye, Trathen, & Schlagel, 2010). And, if you want students to write longer poems, brief acrostic poems are a good way to begin. Start with one-word acrostics and graduate students to writing phrase and sentence acrostics.

- *Writing Free Verse Poetry:* Many students enjoy writing unrhymed, free verse poetry, but a prompt and a formula often give unsure students the help they need. Prompts like "I'm from . . ." or "I wish for . . ." make the ideas and words personal, so students have an easier time with the assignment. Avi, who wrote the "I'm From" poem in Figure 6.4, followed instructions to do a three-part poem with the first part about his neighborhood, the second part about his family, and the third part about himself.

Figure 6.3 *Acrostic poems are one of the easiest types of poems for students to write.*

- *Writing Formula Poetry:* Unlike free verse, where rhyming is not required, many formula poems exist, like haiku, diamante, cinquain, and lantern, with their own specific attributes. Haiku is a Japanese form of poetry

---

"Where I'm From" by Avi S.

I am from paper, CDs and laptops.
I am from soccer balls, bases torn to shreds
and a swing set that glides sideways.
I am from mailboxes, fences, woods behind
    my house,
turning over rocks looking for salamanders.

I am from Jared, Julie, Irving, Myra, Fredda, Robert,
Abraham, Moses and survivors.
I am from get off your PS3, do your homework,
go to sleep now.
From matzo balls, donuts, pizza, latkes,
cake and filet mignon.

I am from Facebook, Youtube, aol, Binghamton news,
Weather.com-tracking storms. I am from the 10
    commandments and
Menorah frames rising high into the air.
I am from keyboards, fingers curved on
    the piano,
notes from my ears—to the song—to the world.

Figure 6.4 *A formula poem shows what matters to this seventh-grade boy.*

Synonym Poems

"Vacation"
Holiday, break, trip or rest
Whatever you call it, it's the best!

"Machines"
Lawn mowers, hair clippers, shredders,
and sharpeners
Everyone uses them including carpenters.

Opposite Poems

What's the opposite of ball?
Something that's straight—not round
at all.

What's the opposite of kind?
Someone who's nasty and mean to
your mind.

Figure 6.5 *Short, easy rhyming poems like these synonym poems and opposite poems are fun to create.*

The Next Step in Vocabulary Instruction © 2012 by Karen Bromley, Scholastic Teaching Resources

that requires a set number of syllables for each of its three lines (five for the first, seven for the second, and five for the third). A lantern poem, also Japanese, is composed of five lines, with a 1–2–3–4–1 pattern. A cinquain, the invention of an American poet inspired by Japanese poetry, contains five lines of two, four, six, eight, and two syllables. These poetry forms focus students on word choices that combine words that sizzle and sparkle with words of specific syllable lengths.

Rhyming poetry like synonym poems, which broaden vocabulary, and opposite poems, which require knowledge of word meanings, can also lead students to write more and longer poems (see Figure 6.5).

ACTIVITY ■ Performance Poetry

Materials: Wham! It's a Poetry Jam by Sara Holbrook (2002)

As well as writing poems, students often delight in performing their own poetry or poems by other people. Performing written poetry with style and pizzazz reinforces vocabulary and fluency, too. *Wham! It's a Poetry Jam* is Sara Holbrook's collection of "call and response" poems, a form of poetry originally used by African poets and storytellers. One person calls out, and a group of people responds in unison. Holbrook says the best thing about these poems is that they give everyone in the audience a chance to be part of the performance without leaving his or her seat.

The lines in Holbrook's poems appear in different colors and fonts to alert speakers to the calls and responses. Holbrook also gives students performance tips on nearly every page of the collection. For example, she says "volume control" is important and explains that "part of a good performance is being loud enough. But always remember, there is a lot of power in talking softly." On the subject of eye contact, she says "When you want to convince someone to see things your way, it's always best to look them in the eye." Holbrook includes more than 30 poems, as well as advice and instructions for putting on a poetry jam at school or in the community.

Extend Your Thinking

Read Paul Janeczko's *Opening Doors: Reading Poetry in the Middle School Classroom* (2003). Janeczko provides detailed lessons for teaching specific poems. Try one of the lessons with a group of middle school students. Was it successful? What would you do differently next time?

ACTIVITY ■ Word Ladders

Materials: Word Ladder reproducible (page 143), pens and pencils

When I heard literacy expert (and prolific writer) Tim Rasinski speak recently, I was especially interested in Word Ladders, one of the wordplay games he shared. This game hooked me immediately because it allows students in grades 1–8 to manipulate letters to make words. This activity requires the use of prior knowledge with a focus on correct spelling. In his series of Daily Word Ladders (2008) that include reproducible pages for different grade levels, Rasinski offers tons of quick and easy vocabulary-building opportunities. On each page, students first read clues that appear on every rung of a ladder.

Then they rearrange and change letters to create words and move up the ladder until they reach the top rung. As students do this, they play with words, analyze sound-symbol relationships, broaden their vocabularies, and build spelling skills to become better readers and writers.

Teaching in Action

I decided to use a Word Ladder to introduce The Wednesday Wars *by Gary Schmidt (2007), a book that my children's literature class would soon be reading. Students in the class were preparing to be classroom teachers, and I wanted to show them an easy word-building game they could use in their own classrooms. At the same time, I introduced the word* wars *from the book's title using the Word Ladder I created (see Figure 6.6).*

To make the clues, I began with the word *wars* on the top rung of the Word Ladder reproducible and wrote the clue "the twentieth century had two of these." Then I changed one letter to make a new word in each descending rung and added a corresponding clue until I reached the bottom rung: 4 letters that mean "to jump." Then students completed this ladder, by moving up one rung at a time until they wrote the last word *wars*. Finally, I asked students to create their own Word Ladder by either beginning at the top or bottom with one word and adding clues. We agreed with Rasinski that a word might change by two or more letters as long as the clue helps students identify it.

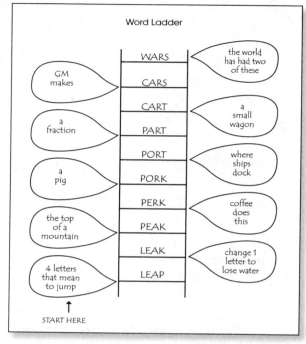

Figure 6.6

Extend Your Thinking

Make a Word Ladder for fourth or fifth graders using a content-area word on either the top or bottom rung. Try your Word Ladder with one or more students and then have the student(s) create a Word Ladder. Do you see any other word-learning benefits of this activity for students?

ACTIVITY ■ **List Swaps**

Materials: lined paper, pens of different colors

Teaching in Action

Jodi, a fifth-grade teacher, used this cooperative learning activity when she noticed three list books on the Internet (see Figure 6.7) and the description of one of them, Falling Down the Page, *caught her eye. To Jodi, list-making sounded like a fun, nonthreatening activity to try with her reluctant writers.*

First, Jodi grouped students in clusters by putting four to six desks together. She gave each group a sheet of lined paper and a pen of a different color. She challenged students to write in 30 seconds as many words as

The Next Step in Vocabulary Instruction © 2012 by Karen Bromley, Scholastic Teaching Resources

they could that related to a topic they were studying or that fit categories she identified, such as space exploration, Florida Everglades, oranges, and marine life. After 30 seconds, Jodi had each group pass its list to the next group, which had 30 seconds to read what was written and add more words. Jodi continued this process until each list returned to the group where it started. After each group had counted the words on its list and read them to the class, Jodi compiled a class list and posted it on a bulletin board for students to reference.

Jodi's students responded so favorably to List Swaps that she now uses it monthly. She says it doesn't just encourage vocabulary building but also encourages correct spelling, because she checks each list and only accepts properly spelled words. Jodi says, "List Swaps is a competitive yet cooperative activity that uses students' oral language to build on their written language. We post the finished lists on a bulletin board so students can use the words when they write reports. We have noticed that legibility improves because everyone sees the final lists."

Extend Your Thinking

Why do you think Jodi give each group a pen of a different color? How might you ensure that one student doesn't take over and do all the writing? How and when would you build in a requirement for proper spelling?

- *Scholastic Book of Lists I* by Robert Stremme & James Buckley, Jr. (Scholastic, 2003)
- *Scholastic Book of Lists II* by Robert Stremme & James Buckley, Jr. (Scholastic, 2007)
- *Falling Down the Page: A Book of List Poems* by Georgia Heard (Ed.) (Roaring Brook Press, 2009).
- *The Book of Lists* by David Wallechinsky and Amy Wallace (Littlehampton Book Services, 1997).

Figure 6.7 *These books show how lists can become poetry.*

ACTIVITY ■ Interview a Word

Materials: container, slips of paper, pen or marker, Interview a Word reproducible (page 144)

This activity requires students to "become" a word as they think about various aspects of a word's meaning, function, and relationship to other words (Bromley, 2002.)

To do the activity, choose several key words from a unit or selection students have read or will read, and model the strategy for the class. You can also have students identify these key words. Then do the following:

1. Create teams of 3–5 students (depending on the number of key vocabulary and class size).
2. Give each team a word and a copy of the Interview a Word reproducible. Or, write the words on slips of paper, place them in a container, and let teams choose one without revealing it to the class.
3. Have each team "become" the word and write answers to the interview questions. Emphasize that students need to pretend they are the word and take its perspective.
4. Encourage students to add humor to their responses and to make the voice of the interviewer dramatic to make the strategy authentic.
5. You or a student can be the interviewer and pose the questions to each team. Team members take turns reading their written answers.

6. After each team interview, have the other teams guess the word. The team that guesses correctly goes next or chooses another team to go next.

Interview a Word is a creative and interesting way to build vocabulary and concept knowledge before or after reading a chapter, selection, unit, or book. Students must use prior knowledge to connect what they already know about a word as they construct new meanings together and use the word in new ways. This activity promotes collaboration and teamwork, which aids learning as students build on each other's knowledge to see how words are related to one another. It also requires that students engage in purposeful listening, speaking, reading, writing, and thinking.

Here are some learning log entries of eighth graders who participated in Interview a Word:

- *"It was fun because I got to work with someone else instead of just writing definitions by myself. My partners and I came up with good ideas about what a word would say and act like if it was a person. When we were done, I knew what the word meant."* (Kelly, age 13)

- *"It made me think more about the word. We had to use our notes and textbook to find out more information about the word. Just writing a definition for a word didn't teach me anything. By looking at the word as a person I had to think really hard about all its relatives."* (Jason, age 14)

- *"We got to research a word and then listen while other kids presented their interviews to the class. This was good because I got to see what other kids came up with and sometimes they looked at a word different than I would. It was a way to review my notes and see how a word is important to the stuff we're studying."* (Josh, age 14)

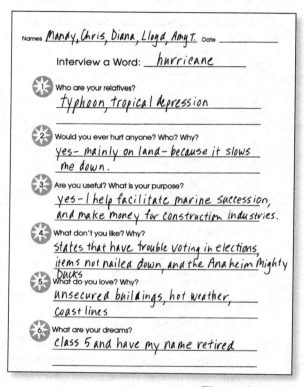

Figure 6.8

ACTIVITY Word Splash

Materials: 25–35 index cards, pencils in different colors, paper and pens or pencils

In this activity, students create a story from several words that fall faceup when a number of word cards are tossed into the air and "splash" down onto the floor or a table (Gautier, 1990). Students must use only the faceup word cards that they can read. The other cards cannot be used. Word Splash is a novel and fun activity that prompts students to be creative as they work with words. Show the class how Word Splash works and have small groups try it.

1. Leaving 8–10 cards blank, write a word from a unit, chapter, or book that students have just read on each of the remaining cards. Words can include nouns, verbs, adjectives, and adverbs with a different color for each part of speech.

The Next Step in Vocabulary Instruction © 2012 by Karen Bromley, Scholastic Teaching Resources

2. Shuffle the cards and toss them into the air, leaving cards as they land, faceup or facedown.

3. Have students discard the facedown cards and arrange the faceup cards in a way that tells what the text was about and/or tells a story.

4. Encourage students to make a sensible story or report from the cards. (They can add words as needed by writing them on any of the blank cards you give them.)

5. Have students read their finished story to the class. Or, have them write it first and then read it to their classmates.

Word Splash offers opportunities for reinforcing vocabulary and developing oral language. When students work together, this activity fosters comprehension, creative thinking, cooperation, and even writing. Some teachers use Word Splash to help students find a writing topic in a random fashion. To do this, after tossing the cards have each student choose a facedown card (one they cannot see) to write about. You may need to collect and toss all the faceup cards several times until every student has been able to choose a facedown card. Students seem to enjoy this random assignment of words, and it is a good way to do a quick writing activity. You might require three sentences, and the entire activity could take less than 10–15 minutes. This helps reinforce vocabulary, and it gives students an opportunity to write a connected text using these important words.

ACTIVITY ■ Quotable Quotes

Materials: computer with Internet access, a selection of quotes

This activity introduces students to unique and humorous opinions and words in quotes related to a specific topic.

Teaching in Action

Wendy, a middle school teacher, wanted to motivate her seemingly uninterested students who had been identified for special help in reading and writing. So, knowing that nearly all of them had a dog or a cat as a pet, she wove this information into a writing activity to support not only their oral vocabulary building but also their reading and writing vocabularies. Wendy talked with students about their pets and shared three of her favorite quotations about dogs from famous and not-so-famous people, which she found on the Internet at www.weforanimals.com/quotations/quotationsdogs.htm:

- *"Whoever said you can't buy happiness forgot about puppies." (Gene Hill)*

- *"What counts is not necessarily the size of the dog in the fight—it's the size of the fight in the dog." (Dwight Eisenhower)*

- *"If your dog is fat, you aren't getting enough exercise." (Unknown)*

This activity helped Wendy's students learn to pronounce previously unknown multisyllabic words (happiness, necessarily, and exercise), and they had fun, too. It was enough to jump-start their interest, and before long Wendy's students had visited several Web sites and read many quotations to one another before filling both bulletin boards outside the classroom with quotations and pictures of dogs and cats. They labeled the bulletin boards "All About Cats" and "People's Best Friends." This activity motivated Wendy's students to use the Internet to search for quotations and pictures, use varied fonts to transcribe the quotations, and create something for others to read.

Quotable Quotes gave these struggling learners opportunities to decode multisyllabic words including *famous, inspirational, collection, memorable, anonymous, unknown,* and *nostalgic.* It required decoding words with inflectional endings, prefixes, and suffixes. Additionally, reading and comprehending the quotations required students to use context to attack unknown words and exposed them to rich language as they read for a real purpose.

ACTIVITY ■ Chat Lingo

Materials: chart paper and marker, computer with Internet access, paper and pens or pencils

Chat Lingo is a fun way to connect digital vocabulary with standard English, and it is motivating for struggling learners and uninterested students because it connects their out-of-school literacies with in-school literacy. This activity taps and builds on students' prior knowledge as it develops their word consciousness. Students practice keyboarding and build their spelling skills, too.

First, show your students a text message like the one below and help them interpret it:

> Hey Opal . . . ty 4 the visit.
>
> Gr8 . . . glad u n wd <3d the pb sndwch.
>
> Did u c the w8 n c tree?
>
> plz come back 2mro. cu then! Glo

> (*Hey Opal, Thank you for the visit.*
>
> *Great, glad you and Winn-Dixie loved the peanut butter sandwich.*
>
> *Did you see the Wait and See Tree?*
>
> *Please come back tomorrow. See you then! Gloria*)

(This is a message from Gloria Dump to Opal, characters in *Because of Winn-Dixie* by Kate DiCamillo (Candlewick, 2000). Opal and her dog, Winn-Dixie, have just visited Gloria Dump. They had a peanut butter sandwich, and Gloria is inviting them to return the next day.)

Next, brainstorm a list of chat lingo, text messaging, and/or Twitter language that students know or use themselves. You can begin with the list in Figure 6.9. Then use abbreviated spellings like BTW, LOL, CU, UR, and so on, and have students produce the standard English to accompany each acronym. To do this, they can collaborate with each other and search the Internet for a text-messaging dictionary that spells out these abbreviations. You can guide students to visit a Web site like www.webopedia.com/quick_ref/textmessageabbreviations.asp, which also includes standard English translations of the abbreviated language. Next, pair students and have each one write a message to a partner in chat or text language from the perspective of a character from a book they are currently reading. Last, have students swap messages and write the chat lingo in standard English.

 The Next Step in Vocabulary Instruction © 2012 by Karen Bromley, Scholastic Teaching Resources

CHAT LINGO, TEXT MESSAGING, AND TWITTER LANGUAGE

?4U	question for you	L8R	later
2MOR	tomorrow	LOL	laughing out loud
AWOL	away without leave	BFN	bye for now
CU	see you	BTW	by the way
BRB	be right back	DYF	did you find?
O4U	only for you	BF	boyfriend
GF	girlfriend	DYK	did you know

Figure 6.9 *These abbreviations make up a new kind of "shorthand."*

Provide Guided Practice

When you have engaged students in direct teaching that involves them in wordplay, enjoying poetry, and writing their own poetry, use these ideas for guided practice that includes fun, humor and the use of lighthearted language.

ACTIVITY ■ Sentence Tag Stories

Materials: pictures cut from magazines or printed from the Internet, paper and pens or pencils
    This activity adds an element of cooperation and fun to story writing.

Teaching in Action

I used Sentence Tag Stories in an after-school program aimed at improving the reading and writing skills of second-, third-, and fourth-grade struggling students. They were reluctant writers who found Sentence Tag Stories an enjoyable and motivating activity. To begin, I explained that the goal was to write a funny or silly story with a partner. To create partnerships, I had students make one long line, and then we folded the line in the middle (>), making two lines side by side with the last child paired with the first child, and so on. This random way of partnering worked well. It gave everyone a buddy and avoided complaints about who would work with whom. Then each pair chose a picture. They examined it together and talked about what may have happened before the picture was taken and after it was taken. Then they used Sentence Tag to write a story together: One partner is "It" and writes the first sentence of the story. Then the other becomes "It" and contributes a sentence to the story. They continue alternating until their story is complete. Ask children to read their stories to the entire group. This shared writing activity, which students saw as play, was so popular that we used it often.

Extend Your Thinking

How could you help struggling elementary schoolchildren use alliteration, rhymes, and similes in their stories? What value do you see in this?

ACTIVITY Words Are Wonderful Day

Materials: chart paper and marker

This activity celebrates novel and unique words in a nonthreatening and fun way. Choose a day of the week and call it "Words Are Wonderful Day" (Cunningham & Allington, 2011). On that day, do different things to celebrate words. Here are some possibilities:

- During your regular read-aloud time, read a wordplay book (page 109) that is lighthearted and extends students' vocabularies at the same time.

- Dress up as a maid (apron and cap) when you read one of the books in the Amelia Bedelia series by Peggy Parish.

- Act out a word for the class to guess.

- Pair students and have them complete a silly crossword puzzle.

- At the end of the day, have students vote to pick one "Wonderful Word" from various words that students nominate. Add that word to a Wonderful Word list and post it in the classroom.

ACTIVITY Calligraphy

Materials: square-nibbed felt-tip calligraphy pens, lined paper, computer with word-processing software program

Calligraphy is the art of creating print that possesses special style and beauty. The word *calligraphy* comes from two Greek words: *kallos,* meaning "beauty," and *graphein,* meaning "to write." Learning calligraphy is a different activity, and it gives students a unique skill that is often used by adults only. Playing with the lettering of words can have a positive effect on students' spelling of academic vocabulary and the legibility of their everyday handwriting. The following comments from fourth-, fifth-, and sixth-grade teachers show some of the reasons they are enthusiastic about doing calligraphy with their students:

- *"I've never before had students ask for time to work on their spelling words."*

- *"Neatness is actually important to them now."*

- *"I can read the writing of students who used to produce some of the most awful work."*

- *"Their vocabulary notebooks are looking better every day."*

- *"It was surprising to see the style carry over to other written work."*

Ask your art teacher to teach students the elements of calligraphy. Or, give each student a square-nibbed felt-tip calligraphy marker and lined paper, and let them experiment. You can also show students the special fonts on their word-processing programs to help them see that there are many different and unique writing styles. Learning calligraphy can even prompt students to research the history of the alphabet, hieroglyphics, rebus writing, pictographs, codes, and ciphers.

The Next Step in Vocabulary Instruction © 2012 by Karen Bromley, Scholastic Teaching Resources

ACTIVITY ◼ **Wikis**

Materials: computer with Internet access

Another form of shared writing occurs when students create a wiki, which is a Web site that allows people to cooperatively create content together. Students can add information and edit each other's work until they have a product they are happy with. At the end of a unit in science or social studies, you might have small groups of students each create a wiki to summarize their learning. Give each group a list of three to five words that represent the important concepts from the unit (or let students determine these words) and have them collaborate to write short reports that include the vocabulary terms and definitions. Tell students to use this vocabulary to frame any questions they have for further investigation.

ACTIVITY ◼ **Word Clouds**

Materials: computer with Internet access

Word clouds are a collection of words related to a particular concept that differ in print size according to their importance. A word cloud gives greater prominence to words that appear more frequently in a text and less prominence to words that appear less frequently. You have probably seen them on the Internet and in magazines. Wordle (www.wordle.net) is a fun, free program that takes text and converts it to a word cloud that looks like digital word art. I

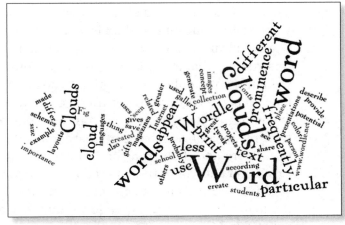

Figure 6.10

created the word cloud in Figure 6.10 by cutting and pasting the text from this paragraph into Wordle. Students can tweak their clouds with different fonts, layouts, and color schemes and create it in different languages. They can print out the images they create, save them to the Wordle gallery to share with others, or use their word clouds on blogs, T-shirts, and wallpaper. To make a word cloud at www.wordle.net, do the following:

1. Click on the "Create" tab at the top of the page.

2. Paste your text in the box or type something directly in the text box.

3. Click "Go" or "Submit," and Wordle will configure your word cloud with a specific design and color scheme.

4. Change the design of the word cloud by clicking "Randomize."

5. Customize it by using the "Font," "Layout," and "Color" tabs above the word cloud.

6. Save your word cloud to the Wordle Gallery and then print it.

Word clouds have great potential to aid students in giving presentations and other school projects. Word clouds require students to type text and choose appropriate, correctly spelled words, or to cut and paste desired text. By emphasizing which words are used most and least often in a given text, word clouds help students see each word's relative importance. Students might use Wordle to create a biographical sketch of a topic or historical time period, an important figure or a character in a book. They might type in a poem, report, or an essay they have written to see how Wordle represents their words. Word clouds also make good gifts when students use words to describe a particular person, place, or thing. They allow students to have fun with words while they learn about how words can represent longer text.

ACTIVITY ■ Idiom Incubator

Materials: a variety of idiom books, container, slips of paper, pen or marker

English idioms are a source of great confusion for ELLs. An idiom is a phrase or sentence whose actual meaning differs from its literal meaning. Idioms are confusing because many words in English have multiple meanings. For instance, *bridge* can mean "a card game," "a structure that spans water," or "a row of replacement teeth." Confusion results when a student knows only the definition "a structure that spans water" and hears or reads "She likes to play *bridge* with her friends," so, teaching students the multiple meanings of words is important. Remember from your previous reading that 70 percent of common words have multiple meanings. Literature that highlights idioms, and the humor that results when people misunderstand them, is a good way to alert students to idioms.

As you and your students read these books, find idioms in them and talk about them. Have students write them on slips of paper, then collect the slips in a word jar or box labeled "Idiom Incubator." When you have a few minutes between lessons or at the end of the day, have a volunteer pull an idiom from the incubator, in which the number of idioms has been increasing (because an incubator helps things grow!). The student then reads the idiom to the class and

---

IDIOM BOOKS

These books help ELLs learn about idioms.

- *Amelia Bedelia's First Apple Pie* by Herman Parish (HarperCollins, 2010)
- *Amelia Bedelia's First Valentine* by Herman Parish (HarperCollins, 2009)
- *Amelia Bedelia's First Day of School* by Herman Parish (HarperCollins, 2009)
- *Super Silly Sayings That Are Over Your Head: A Children's Illustrated Book of Idioms* by Catherine Snodgrass (Starfish Specialty Press, 2004)
- *Scholastic Dictionary of Idioms* (revised) by Marvin Terban (Scholastic, 2006)
- *In a Pickle and Other Funny Idioms* by Marvin Terban and Giulio Maestro (Scholastic, 2007)
- *The One and Only Sam: A Story Explaining Idioms for Children With Asperger Syndrome and Other Communication Difficulties* by Aileen Stalker (Jessica Kingsley Pub, 2009)
- *Mad as a Wet Hen!: And Other Funny Idioms* by Marvin Terban and Giulio Maestro (Scholastic, 2007)

The Next Step in Vocabulary Instruction © 2012 by Karen Bromley, Scholastic Teaching Resources

calls on someone to supply an interpretation. In this way, students can review the idioms they have met and remind themselves of their real meanings. Idioms in the Idiom Incubator can also serve as story starters for creative writing that can be fun for students of all ages. For example, students can illustrate an idiom book with pictures of the idiom's literal meaning and an explanation of what it really means.

> ### Extend Your Thinking
>
> Read one of the idiom books listed on page 122 to a group of students. Which idioms are they aware of and which ones give them trouble? Read *Idioms and Other English Expressions* (books for grades 1–3 and 4–6) by Tim Rasinski, Kathleen Knoblock, and Kathleen Kopp (Shell Education, 2008) for ideas that introduce students to hyperbole, simile, metaphor, and personification.

ACTIVITY ■ Book Jackdaw

Materials: 3-inch by 5-inch index cards, markers, container

This activity, in which students find objects or artifacts to represent a book they have just read, develops vocabulary, storytelling abilities, and confidence in talking about books via concrete objects. A jackdaw is a bird similar to a grackle that collects bright objects in its nest. Book Jackdaw is a classroom collection of items that reflects the content of a specific book.

Before reading a book to the class, show students a jackdaw you created for the book. For example, objects to represent key ideas in *Maniac Magee* by Jerry Spinelli (Scholastic, 1990) might include a shoe lace (to represent his running), a baseball (to represent an important sport in the story), an M&Ms wrapper (to represent Maniac's initials), and a MARS bar wrapper (to represent Maniac's adversary). The objects could be contained in a shoebox (to represent Maniac's penchant for running). Attach a label with the word for each object and include something you have written about the book, too. As you show each object to the class, tell a little bit about how it fits the story without giving too much away to build interest in the book. Then have students make their own book jackdaw for a book they have read or are reading independently, and share it with the class. Be sure to have students include a written artifact (a poem, ad, character sketch, diary entry, or a letter to the author). Book jackdaws are an alternative to traditional book reports. Displaying book jackdaws (on tables or a windowsill) can motivate students to examine them, learn new words, and read each other's books.

ACTIVITY ■ Scavenger Hunt

Materials: objects and clues for scavenger hunt

Scavenger hunts are another active, entertaining tool for word learning. They are a novel and fun way to expand students' vocabularies and world knowledge. In a scavenger hunt, teams of students have a list of words and must find objects or pictures to represent them in a given amount of time. The team that finds the most things wins.

Teaching in Action

Tanisha tried a classroom scavenger hunt with her sixth graders, and they loved it. She used words from the book they had just read, What a Great Idea!: Inventions That Changed the World *by Stephen Tomachek (2003).*

Because of her students' energetic response to this scavenger hunt, Tanisha decided to use one several times a year to accompany a content unit or a book the class was reading. It turned out to be a hit with her students, who became clever at hunting and creating. She says, "There are three things that make scavenger hunts a great word-learning tool. First, the students really learn a lot of words as they listen and watch each other explain how different items can represent a word. Second, their sight and meaning vocabularies grow. Third, as they work together in teams, they learn how to help each other and appreciate each other's ingenuity."

Extend Your Thinking

What problems might arise with scavenger hunts, and how might you plan ahead to avoid them?

DIRECTIONS FOR THE SCAVENGER HUNT ACTIVITY

1. Choose a topic the class has studied or a book the students will read.

2. List important words from the topic or a book. (from *What a Great Idea!: Inventions That Changed the World*)

pottery	clock	steam engine	battery	axle	airplane	anesthesia
telegraph	irrigation	compass	camera	antiseptic	phonograph	waterwheels
microscope	light bulb	maps	telescope	x-ray	rocket	antibiotics
computer	transistor	laser	plastic	fertilizer	nuclear reactor	

3. Explain what a scavenger hunt is, divide the class into teams, and give each team a list of the words.

4. Give teams a week to gather objects or pictures and/or drawings to represent words. Tell them that items will earn two points and pictures or drawings will earn one point.

5. Let teams meet to discuss how to find a word's meaning, how to represent the word, and who will scavenge for each word.

6. Provide time during the week for teams to discuss their progress.

7. On the last day, have members explain why and how objects and/or pictures represent each word, and record points as teams share scavenged items.

8. Have students create a bulletin board with each team's printed words and pictures and a title to represent them (e.g." Inventions That Changed the World.") Display labeled items nearby.

Try Independent Activities

Here are several ideas for students to pursue on their own as they explore independently, and/or with family members, other avenues for building vocabulary.

- **Commercial Word Games:** There are many interactive educational games that build vocabulary. The list on the next page is a good one to send home to parents in your weekly or monthly newsletter. You might feature one game in each newsletter so as not to overpower parents with too much information at once. These games are fun and can build the entire family's vocabulary and concept knowledge in enjoyable ways. Word games make good birthday and holiday gifts for all students, not just those who struggle with expanding their vocabularies.

COMMERCIAL WORD GAMES

- *ASAP:* (University Games) (ages 8 and up) Fast, furious, and fun, this game requires quick thinking and talking in 26 categories.

- *Balderdash:* (Mattel) (ages 10 and up) This bluffing game has others "call your bluff." Categories contain unbelievable but true statements about people, words, initials, movies, and laws. Players make up answers and read them along with the correct one, then vote to choose the "real" answer. They score points for guessing correctly and for bluffing the other players.

- *Bella's Mystery Deck:* (MindWare) (ages 10–12) There are 50 mini-mysteries in the deck of cards. Players read to find clues needed to uncover secrets, spot phony alibis, and catch crooks. Answers are printed at the end of each mystery, and players use a mirror card to read them.

- *Blurt:* (Patch Products) (ages 7 and up) The object of Blurt is to be the first person to blurt out the correct word: "What is the last car on a freight train?" "Caboose!" Right, but you've got to think faster. Blurt is a fun party game for adults and a great vocabulary builder for kids.

- *Boggle:* (Parker Brothers) (ages 8 and up) Players have three minutes to shake lettered cubes, drop them into a grid, and start a timer before guessing words, then racing to see who can list the most words with the highest point value.

- *Catch Phrase:* (Parker Brothers) (ages 8 and up) The players in the "Catch it, … Say it, … Pass it" game do whatever it takes to get their team to say the word shown.

- *Gramopoly:* (Lingui Systems) (ages 10–15) Each player is assigned a sentence from three levels of difficulty. Players must purchase parts of speech to complete their sentence. This game teaches nouns, pronouns, adverbs, adjectives, verbs, articles, conjunctions, helping verbs, prepositional phrases, and interjections.

- *Parts of Speech Bingo:* (Trend) (ages 7–11) These bingo games are fun, fast-paced, and feature five different game versions. Players learn parts of speech and how they are used. The game includes a caller's mat and corresponding cards, answer sheet, 36 game boards, and more than 250 markers.

- *Password:* (Endless Games) (ages 8 and up) In this classic word-association game, teams of two players compete to see who's the fastest at guessing the correct password.

- *Pictionary:* (Milton Bradley) (ages 8–adult) Teammates must guess a secret word before time runs out. The game includes a challenge die with other game variations.

- *Pictionary Jr.:* (Milton Bradley) (ages 7–12) Players sketch items for teammates to guess in a minute or less.

- *Quiddler:* (SET Enterprises) (ages 8 and up) Players combine letters into words using letters with the highest point value. Players first use three cards (round one), then four, on up to ten cards in the last round.

- *Scattergories:* (Milton Bradley) (ages 8 and up) Players try to match categories using words that start with the same letter. Points are scored if no other player matches your answers.

- *Scrabble:* (Milton Bradley) (ages 8 and up) Players use seven letters to build crosswords and get bonus spaces to add to their scores.

- *Smart Mouth:* (Binary Arts) (ages 8 and up) In this quick-thinking word game, players go head to head in a fast-paced free-for-all. You can play individually or in teams.

- *Tribond:* (Patch Products) (ages 8 and up) Quick: what do "A Wave," "A Split-Fingered Fastball," and "A Huddle" have in common? If you answered "They all break," then you solved a problem. Tribond includes clues in five categories, multiple-choice surprises, and original questions. (Tribond Jr. is for ages 7 and up).

- *Up for Grabs:* (Tyco) (ages 8 and up) Players must create or steal as many scoring words as possible by making new words from the tiles that are flipped over or by "grabbing" a word by adding a letter to it to form a new word.

- *Upwords:* (Milton Bradley) (ages 10 and up) In this three-dimensional crossword game, players create words by building on tiles already on the board.

- *Wordopoly:* (Lingui Systems) (ages 10–15) This game seeks to improve students' word use and vocabulary skills with a Monopoly-style approach.

- *Word Sense:* (Binary Arts) (ages 10 and up) Players take turns flipping letter tiles and racing to think of words that contain those letters. For example, flip S-P-O, and call out STOP, POSTER, PREPOSTEROUS, or OPPOSITE. The first to correctly call out a word gets to keep the tiles. The player with the most points at the end is the winner.

- *Writeopoly:* (Lingui Systems) (ages 9–14) Players improve their written language skills by traveling around a colorful game board buying properties (Character, Setting, Type of Writing) and filling out Writing Plan sheets. When the game is over, players are ready to complete an original piece of writing.

- **Online Word Games:** The list of games on the next page is similar to the Commercial Word Games list, but it also includes Web sites for vocabulary-building games. The games described on page 128 are free game apps for smartphones and iPads. You might include the name and description of an online word game and a free app in each newsletter you send home. Some teachers post this kind of list near classroom computers so students can easily find a site for vocabulary building fun when they have time. Again, these games allow students to play with words and learn more about language in nonthreatening and enjoyable ways.

Online word games such as "Eat Your Words, "Word Hunt," "Word Drop," and "Word Sudoku" are available from Merriam-Webster at www.merriam-webster.com/game/index.htm. There are also daily crossword puzzles and Scrabble, both of which heighten students' awareness of spelling and the meanings of words. "Unscramble," "Hang Mouse," "Clueless Words," "Oxymorons," and "Hig Pigs" are few of the vocabulary games you can find at www.vocabulary.co.il, where you will also find online foreign-language games and ELL games. These are a great way to begin to learn another language. Students and adults alike love learning foreign words and phrases using the matching games at this site.

Extend Your Thinking

Read "eVoc Strategies: 10 Ways to Use Technology to Build Vocabulary" by Bridget Dalton and Dana Grisham in *The Reading Teacher, 64*(1), 2011. Try one of these activities yourself first and then use it with a group of students. What did you learn? What did they learn?

ONLINE WORD GAMES

- www.vocabulary.com: features puzzles and games to help build vocabulary; enables students to earn a diploma from "Vocabulary University"

- www.gamequarium.com/spanishvocab.html: suggests links to many Spanish vocabulary games that teach words related to such categories as animals, people, food, weather, and so on

- www.surfnetkids.com/dictionary.htm: contains descriptions and links to several online dictionaries for students

- www.merriam-webster.com/game: offers a different "Word Game of the Day" in one of several different puzzle formats and an easy-to-use thesaurus

- www.eduplace.com/tales: provides "Wacky Web Tales" that students can complete by supplying 10–15 words for various parts of speech (a plural noun, a large number, an adjective, and so on) and publishes these stories

- www.acronymfinder.com/about.asp#what: searches for, expands, and provides meanings for acronyms like NASA and NATO

- http://games.funschool.com: offers more than 30 vocabulary and number games

- www.edhelper.com/vocabulary.htm: creates worksheets when students supply a list of spelling words, and also offers activities with roots and affixes

- http://superkids.com/aweb/tools/words: offers six vocabulary games including "Word of the Day," "Hangman," "Hidden Word Puzzles," and "Word Scramblers"

- http://myvocabulary.com: features grade-level puzzles, thematic interactive puzzles, and student-created vocabulary stories

- http://boardgames.lovetoknow.com/Games_Scrabble%2C_Password%2C_and_Pictionary_as_Vocabulary_Tools: has board games that add interest and challenge to learning and reinforcing targeted vocabulary words

FREE APPS FOR SMARTPHONES AND IPADS

Word Lens	Camera application that translates pictures and words
Word Warp	Timed game. Player uses 6 letters to make words.
Word Popper	Timed game. Player uses 27 letters to make words.
Word Squares	Player arranges 16 letters on a board to spell words both horizontally and vertically

ACTIVITY ■ Unusual Words Search

Materials: small notebooks (or paper) and pens or pencils

This after-school homework activity is a modification of the scavenger hunt idea. You can challenge your students to search for unique and unusual word use in a setting outside of school and give them extra credit in their language arts class for completing this assignment. Share the following directions with them:

- Visit a setting outside of school (a store, business, or other public place).

- Make a list of any unique or unusual vocabulary you find in that setting.

- Bring the list to school and share it with your classmates—but do not name the setting where you found the words.

- Have your classmates guess the setting.

Teaching in Action

Scott tried this activity with his sixth graders, and three students shared their lists in class (see Figure 6.11). List #1 contains words that a girl and her father came up with after going to a baseball game together and talking to a baseball player. List #2 contains words that a girl found on the labels of hair treatment products in a beauty salon. List #3 words came from boxes of golf balls that a boy found in a sporting goods store.

Older students enjoy searching for unusual and unique words in the environment. This activity exposes struggling learners to rich language and builds their word consciousness. They become independent word learners as their awareness and knowledge of advertising and marketing grows. "Unusual Ad Words" can be a popular out-of-school activity with your students, too. When you encourage family involvement, parents will often take their children to visit places in the community they might not normally visit.

The Next Step in Vocabulary Instruction © 2012 by Karen Bromley, Scholastic Teaching Resources

UNUSUAL WORDS SEARCH

List #1 (baseball game)	List #2 (beauty shop)	List #3 (sporting goods store: boxes of golf balls)
Baltimore chop	Head Banger	LoCo
assist	Bad Toys	Feel Speed
can of corn	Creative Genius	Big Results
slurve	Curls Rock	Scary Long
changeup	Fast Fixed	More Carry
line out	Root Boost	Noodle
golden sombrero		

Figure 6.11 *These students looked for unique vocabulary and found these words in three different settings.*

ACTIVITY ■ Alphabet Acronyms

Materials: computer with Internet access, paper and pens or pencils

This activity engages students in searching the Internet to find the words that certain acronyms stand for.

Teaching in Action

Sandy, a middle school ELL teacher, knows that many of his students love using the computer. So he gives them a list of several well-known American acronyms, such as SCUBA and NASA, and initialisms, such as TV, CBS, NBC, PBS, BMW, NBA, NFL, KFC, VIP, and RIP, and has students work in pairs to search the Internet for the words that represent these terms. This activity quickly teaches students the letters of the alphabet and the words they stand for. Sandy also has students label vowels and consonants to familiarize them with English spelling. He calls Alphabet Acronyms "a fun and challenging activity for beginning ELLs who are not yet even aware that they already know many letters of the alphabet. As they soon discover, they are aware of American logos and initialisms and acronyms, particularly from the sports and entertainment fields."

This activity exposes struggling learners to everyday acronyms that are often perceived as being words themselves. Additionally, determining what an acronym stands for by searching the Internet helps these students become independent readers. Students who want an extra challenge can create a bulletin board or a PowerPoint presentation to share their findings. They can create a bulletin board that holds their findings and/or share their acronyms, pictures, and words with classmates.

ACTIVITY ■ AWAD

Materials: computer with Internet access

A-Word-a-Day (AWAD) (www.wordsmith.org/awad/index.html) sends a daily e-mail to subscribers with a new word appropriate for upper-grade and/or middle school students. AWAD includes a vocabulary word, its definition, pronunciation information (including an audio clip), etymology, a usage example, an example of the word used in a sentence, and other interesting tidbits about words. Words are usually selected around a weekly theme. You and/or your students can subscribe to a free edition and receive it automatically.

One of the tidbits I discovered from a 2010 AWAD posting is that text messaging language is not a new phenomenon. Hundreds of years ago, Victorian poets such as Charles Bombaugh used numbers and the sounds of letters to represent words. In 1867, 130 years before the arrival of mobile phone texting, Bombaugh used the phrase "I wrote 2 U B 4," and another verse read, "He says he loves U 2 X S/ U R virtuous and Y's." (He says he loves you to excess. You are virtuous and wise.) Many students today have figured out that they can sign off an email or text message as LN (Ellen), ME (Emmy), KC (Casey), J (Jay), LX (Alex), KT (Katie), or K8 (Kate).

ACTIVITY ■ Vacation Vocabulary

Materials: LaRue Across America: Postcards From the Vacation by Mark Teague (Scholastic, 2011), 5-inch by 8-inch tag board, markers, U.S. and world maps, yarn

In this activity, students write short, humorous entries on postcards from places they visited during their summer vacation or holiday vacation. They can do this activity independently at home with or without the help of parents or siblings. It improves their knowledge of geography and proper nouns for cities, states, and recreation areas.

Make a postcard out of tag board; draw a stamp and add lines for an address and a written message. The blank side is where students can draw a picture of the place they visited or a site they saw.

Begin the activity by reading *LaRue Across America: Postcards From the Vacation* to your students. This book contains postcards from Ike, a dog who has gone on vacation with some cats. Ike writes postcards to a neighbor, Mrs. Hibbins, about his escapades as they travel together. Then give each student a postcard or two to complete and bring back to the classroom. Ask students to read their cards to one another and then collect them on a bulletin board. Use pins or tacks and yarn to connect each postcard to the place on a map where different students visited. This is a novel way to build geography knowledge, celebrate students' recreational lives, and encourage them to have fun writing short descriptive messages.

ACTIVITY ■ 10 Best Ideas for Parents

Materials: 10 Best Ways for Parents to Build Vocabulary

Out of 168 hours in a week, students spend only about 35 hours in school. So, as much as you can do in school in the limited amount of time you have, parents certainly have a lot more time with their children. It makes sense then to enlist parents' help in activities that are lighthearted

10 BEST WAYS FOR PARENTS TO BUILD VOCABULARY

Send these ideas home to get parent support for vocabulary building.

1. Talk a little and listen a lot. Children's language grows from listening and speaking, as well as from reading and writing. So give kids of all ages lots of opportunities to talk, question, observe, and have conversations with you.

2. Jazz up your language. Use words like *huge* and *enormous* rather than *big*. You are a model, and your child learns from you.

3. Read daily with your child. Whether you take turns reading a book together for 15 minutes, share newspaper headlines or an interesting article, make oral reading a daily family habit. Oral reading introduces your child to new words and concepts.

4. Decorate your refrigerator. Purchase magnetic letters or words. Putting letters together to make words builds spelling and word-recognition skills, as well as vocabulary skills.

5. Keep pencils, pens and paper handy. Encouraging your child to help you make a grocery list, take telephone messages, and write notes to family members helps build written vocabulary skills.

6. Hire an "assistant cook." Reading labels and recipes and following directions help children add useful words to their vocabulary while learning the valuable skill of food preparation when they help you make meals.

7. Use the Internet. With proper supervision, children can stretch their vocabulary by volumes online. Discussion boards, e-mail, chat rooms, and instant messaging all require children to learn and use words to communicate. Search the term "vocabulary games" and you'll be surprised what you find!

8. Visit the library together. There are scads of magazines, audiotapes, and books for you and your child. And they're all free (your tax dollars at work!).

9. Take delight in language. Note unique words and phrases, as well as beautiful and powerful uses of language. Notice acronyms and what they stand for. Poetry is full of images that give words life, so read poems together.

10. Use a dictionary. Science, social studies, and math are hard for many kids because of the technical vocabulary. Dictionaries help unlock these hard words. Even everyday words give kids problems (70 percent have more than one meaning), so bookmark an online dictionary.

Plus—See the world through a new lens. Help your child be a "word worm" or "word wizard" by reading the world together. Stretch your child's vocabulary by reading billboards, street signs, maps, TV guides, menus, movie reviews, game directions, posters, books, magazines, cereal boxes, and everything else in the environment.

and fun and can develop students' vocabulary and language. See the list on page 131 for ten great ways to help parents sneak word learning into their daily routines at home. Share this list in your newsletter and/or give it to parents during open house or curriculum night.

Daily Calendar: Chocolate

These activities are a blend of online and paper-and-pencil tasks that are fun but also teach students about this popular food. Many people are passionate about chocolate because of its sensational taste. If parents don't have Internet access at home or at school, they can go to their public library and use the computers there to do the activities in this list.

DAILY CALENDAR: CHOCOLATE

Week 1: Getting Started

1. **Have students look up** the words *chocolate* and *carob* in a dictionary to find out what each word means and how they are alike and different. Can you substitute one for the other, and do they have the same taste and texture?

2. **Ask students** to make a list of all the foods they can think of that contain chocolate. Have them think about cereal, muffins, cookies, candy bars, and beverages. They should have at least ten items on their lists, and if they really think hard, they could go to 25 or more!

3. **Encourage students** to visit a grocery store and look for chocolate on the shelves in the baking goods aisle. Ask them to find as many different flavors and kinds of chocolate as they can and report what they found back to the class.

4. **Have students visit** en.wikipedia.org/wiki/Cacao_bean to read about the cocoa bean and chocolate. They can find pictures of cacao trees and pods, and read about where two-thirds of the world's cocoa is produced.

5. **Have students draw** pictures of a cocoa tree with cacao beans growing on it. Encourage them to use colored markers, pencils, or paint. Have them revisit the Web site above if they can't remember the leaves, bark, and pods.

Week 2: Exploring Chocolate

6. **Ask students** to visit www.hersheys.com and browse it to see what kinds of information it provides. Have students click on "Recipes" and find one they would like to make and then print the recipe and take it home to make.

7. **Read a book** about chocolate to your class, a chapter a day. Ask your school's library-media specialist to find several books on chocolate. Choose one and put the rest on display for students to read in their free time. Two possibilities are *Charlie and the Chocolate Factory* by Roald Dahl (2001) and *Chocolate Fever* by Robert Kimmel Smith (1972).

8. **Invite a dietician** or an older student taking a home-and-careers class to talk to your students about the nutritional components in chocolate and its place in the food pyramid. Ask him or her to discuss the benefits of a balanced diet and talk about what constitutes junk food.

9. **Find out** with your class what the Ms in M&M's® candy stand for. Why did the inventors of this popular candy create M&M's in the first place? How has their product changed over the years?

10. **Discover** the different kinds of chocolate candy that Mars, Inc. makes when you and your students visit Mars.com. What other products does the company make? Why do you think it makes such a variety of foods?

Week 3: Delving Deeper

11. **Build math skills** (multiplication, counting, and sets) by reading *The Hershey's Milk Chocolate Multiplication Book* by Jerry Pallotta (2002) or *The M & M's Brand Chocolate Candies Counting Book* (1994) by Barbara McGrath to your class (depending on your students' math level).

12. **Visit** www.marsbotanical.com with your class and click on "About" to find out what "flavanols" are and why the Mars company is doing research on them.

13. **Take a video tour** of a chocolate factory with your class and follow a chocolate bean until it becomes a chocolate bar when you visit Exploratorium magazine at www.exploratorium.edu/exploring/exploring_chocolate/.

14. **Encourage students** to draw pictures that show the sequence of events they saw at the Web site above. Have them add key words and arrows to label the journey from bean to candy bar. Share this picture and the one they did of a cacao tree with all your students or another class.

15. **Ask your school's library-media specialist** to find books about chocolate for your students to read to younger children. Two possibilities are *Chocolatina* by Eric Kraft (2008) and *Curious George Goes to a Chocolate Factory* by Margaret Rey (1998). Have students practice reading before you pair them with younger children.

Week 4: Going Beyond

16. **Play Making Words With Names** (page 15) with the word *chocolate* by having your students work in pairs to make as many small words as they can by rearranging the letters in chocolate. (They should be able to make at least 15 words).

17. **Collect menus** from local restaurants. Help your students examine the foods and beverages listed on them for items that contain chocolate. Note the descriptive language used to sell these and other items. Compare what is sold in different restaurants, how it is marketed, and what it costs.

18. **Invite the director** of your school cafeteria to talk to your class about the four basic food groups and examples of foods from each one. Help students compare the nutritional values and food groups of various fruits, cookies, cakes, puddings, breads, and other foods they eat in a cafeteria lunch.

19. **Have students collect** labels from various prepackaged foods (including those with chocolate). Make a bulletin board into a data chart by listing foods down the left side and nutritional categories printed on most packaged foods in columns across the top. Help students compare the nutritional values of foods they eat.

20. **Estimate the number** of M&M's in a small bag (individual size) with your class. Have each student open a small bag, sort the candies by color, and count them to see how close their estimation was. Have students count the number of each color and make a circle graph or bar graph to show this. Compare these graphs as students eat their M&M's!

Week 5: Mmmmmore About Chocolate

21. **Have students collect** wrappers from several chocolate candy bars. Help them examine and compare the prices, nutritional components, and percentages of fat, carbohydrates, protein, and sugar in each. What conclusions can they make?

22. **Encourage imagination** and storytelling with a "Round the Class" story about chocolate. First, read *Cloudy With a Chance of Meatballs* by Judi Barrett (1978) to the class. Then start your own story—*Cloudy With a Chance of Chocolate Chips*—and have students take turns telling parts of it.

23. **Ask parents** to send in their child's favorite chocolate recipe. Have each student copy his or her recipe and add an illustration for a class Chocolate Cookbook. Include a table of contents with the names of the desserts and students' names. Reproduce it for everyone. (It could be a Mother's Day gift!)

24. **Have students use** collage materials to make a picture of the special chocolate confection they created yesterday. Decorate a "Unique Chocolate Confections" bulletin board with these pictures and add the names and descriptions each student created.

25. **Have students create** an acrostic for the word *chocolate* by including all the words they can think of that begin with each letter. First, brainstorm a list of words to describe how chocolate looks, smells, feels, and tastes. Have students share their acrostic poetry.

Going Way Beyond

26. **Visit** virtualchocolate.com and have your students send virtual postcards of chocolaty greetings to friends. At this site they can also read chocolate quotes, download chocolate pictures for their computer screens, and write their own chocolate quote or comment.

27. **Have students write** letters to the author of the chapter book you read to them this month. Send them to the publisher and ask that they be forwarded to the author. Suggest that students tell what they liked or didn't like about the book and if they have an idea for a sequel.

28. **Plan** a hot cocoa party with your class and another class. Make hot chocolate for everyone and have your students share some of the writing they have done, artwork they have created, and things they have learned about chocolate this month.

Finally . . .

"Why is six afraid of seven?" "Because seven eight (ate) nine!" Wordplay activities like the ones in this book offer you many ways to build students' vocabulary. Providing the direct instruction, guided collaborative practice, and independent activities suggested in these pages is critical to developing your students' comprehension, fluency, and independence. Better vocabulary instruction can be a challenge, but it's well worth it when the result is word learners who are able to learn across the curriculum!

References

Bear, D. R., Helman, L. A., & Woessner, L. (2009). Word study assessment and instruction with ELLs in a second-grade classroom: Bending with students' growth. In Coppola, J., & Primas, E. V. (Eds.), *One classroom, many learners: Best literacy practices for today's multilingual classrooms.* Newark, DE: International Reading Association (pp. 11–40).

Bear, D. R., Invernizzi, M., Templeton, S., & Johnston, F. (2011). *Words their way: Word study for phonics, vocabulary, and spelling instruction* (5th ed.). Upper Saddle River, NJ: Pearson.

Beck, I. L., & McKeown, M. G. (2007). Increasing young low-income children's oral vocabulary repertoires through rich and focused instruction. *Elementary School Journal, 107*(3), 251–272.

Beck, I. L., McKeown, M. G., & Kucan, L. (2002). *Bringing words to life: Robust vocabulary instruction.* New York: Guilford.

Berne, J. I., & Blachowicz, C. L. (2008). What reading teachers say about vocabulary instruction: Voices from the classroom. *The Reading Teacher, 62*(4), 314–323.

Blachowicz, C., & Fisher, P. J. (2002). *Teaching vocabulary in all classrooms* (2nd ed.). Upper Saddle River, NJ: Merrill-Prentice Hall.

Blevins, W. (1998). Make the most of phonograms. *Instructor*, p. 74.

Bromley, K. (2002). *Stretching students' vocabulary.* New York: Scholastic.

Bromley, K. (2007). 9 things every teacher should know about words and vocabulary instruction. *Journal of Adolescent and Adult Literacy, 50*(7), 528–539.

Cambourne, B. (1988). *The whole story: Natural learning and the acquisition of literacy in the classroom.* Auckland, NZ: Scholastic.

Common core state standards for ELA (2011). Retrieved from www.corestandards.org.

Cunningham, P. M. (2009). *What really matters in vocabulary: Research-based practices across the curriculum.* Boston: Pearson.

Cunningham, P. M., & Allington, R. L. (2011). *Classrooms that work: They can all read and write* (5th ed.). Upper Saddle River, NJ: Pearson.

Ehri, L. C., & Rosenthal, J. (2007). Spellings of words: A neglected facilitator of vocabulary learning. *Journal of Literacy Research, 39*(4), 389–409.

Fisher, D., & Frey, N. (2008). *Word wise and content rich: Five essential steps to teaching academic vocabulary.* Portsmouth, NH: Heinemann.

Frye, E. M., Trathen, W., & Schlagel, B. (2010). Extending acrostic poetry into content learning: A scaffolding framework. *The Reading Teacher, 63*(7), 591–595.

Fuchs, L. S., Fuchs, D., Hosp, M. K., & Jenkins, J. R. (2001). Oral reading fluency as an indicator of reading competence: A theoretical, empirical, and historical analysis. *Scientific Studies of Reading, 5*(3), 239–256.

Gardner, H. (2000). *Intelligence reframed: Multiple intelligences for the 21st century.* New York: Basic Books.

Gautier, L. R. (1990). Word Splash. *Reading Teacher, 44*(2), 184.

Graves, M. F. (2006). *The vocabulary book: Learning and instruction.* New York: Teachers College Press.

Graves, M. F., & Watts-Taffee, S. M. (2002). The place of word consciousness in a research-based vocabulary program. In A. E. Farstrup & S. J. Samuels (Eds.), *What research has to say about vocabulary instruction* (3rd ed.). Newark, DE: International Reading Association, 140–165.

Harmon, J. (2002). Teaching independent word learning strategies to struggling readers. *Journal of Adolescent and Adult Literacy, 45*(7), 606–615.

Harmon, J. M., & Hedrick, W. B. (2000). Zooming in and zooming out: Enhancing vocabulary and conceptual learning in social studies. *The Reading Teacher, 54*(2), 155–159.

Hart, B., & Risley, T. R. (1995). *Meaningful differences in the everyday experience of young American children.* Baltimore, MD: Brooks.

Heisey, N., & Kucan, L. (2010). Introducing science concepts to primary students through read-alouds: Interactions and multiple texts make the difference. *The Reading Teacher, 63*(8), 666–676.

Hopkins, G., & Bean T. W. (1999). Vocabulary learning with the verbal-word association strategy in a Native American community. *Journal of Adolescent & Adult Literacy, 42*(4), 274–281.

Hoyt, L. (1999). *Revisit, reflect, retell: Strategies for improving reading comprehension.* Portsmouth, NH: Heinemann.

Janeczko, P. B. (1999). *How to write poetry.* New York: Scholastic.

Keene, E. O., & Zimmerman, S. (2007). *Mosaic of thought: The power of comprehension strategy instruction* (2nd ed.). Portsmouth, NH: Heinemann.

Kelley, J. G., Lesaux, N. K., Kieffer, M. J., & Faller, S. E. (2010). Effective academic vocabulary instruction in the urban middle school. *The Reading Teacher, 64*(1), 5–14.

Kelly, M. J., & Clausen-Grace, N. (2010). Guiding students through expository text with text feature walks. *The Reading Teacher, 64,* 191–195.

Lane, H. B., & Allen, S. A. (2010). The vocabulary-rich classroom: Modeling sophisticated word use to promote word consciousness and vocabulary growth. *The Reading Teacher, 63*(5), 362–370.

Lederer, R. (1991). *The miracle of language.* New York: Pocket Books.

McGhee, P. E. (1984). Play, incongruity and humor. In T. Yawkey, & A. Pellegrini (Eds.), *Child's play: Developmental and applied* (pp. 219–236). Mahwah, NJ: Lawrence Erlbaum.

Manyak, P. C., & Bauer, E. B. (2009). English vocabulary instruction for English learners. *The Reading Teacher, 63*(2), 174–176.

Marzano, R. J., & Pickering, D. J. (2005). *Building academic vocabulary: Teacher's manual.* Alexandria, VA: Association for Supervision and Curriculum Development.

Moats, L. C. (2000). *Speech to print: Language essentials for teachers.* Baltimore: Brookes.

Mountain, L. (2005). Rooting out meaning: More morphemic analysis for primary pupils. *The Reading Teacher, 58*(8), 742–749.

Mountain, L. (2002). Flip-a-chip to build vocabulary. *Journal of Adolescent and Adult Literacy,* 62–68.

Nagy, W. E., & Scott, J. (2000). Vocabulary processes. In M. L. Kamil, P. B. Mosenthal, P. D. Pearson, & R. Barr (Eds.), *Handbook of reading research, 3*(269–284) Mahwah, NJ: Lawrence Erlbaum.

Oczkus, L. (2010). *Reciprocal teaching at work, K–12* (2nd ed.). Newark, DE: International Reading Association.

Paivio, A. (1990). *Mental representations: A dual-coding approach.* New York: Oxford University Press.

Pexman, P. M., Glenwright, M., Krol, A., & James, T. (2005). An Acquired Taste: Children's Perceptions of Humor and Teasing in Verbal Irony. *Discourse Processes: A Multidisciplinary Journal, 40*(3), 259–288.

Raphael, T. (1986). Teaching question-answer relationships, revisited. *The Reading Teacher, 39* (516–622).

Rasinski, T. (2008). *Daily word ladders (Gr. 1–2, 2–3, and 4–6).* New York: Scholastic.

Rasinski, T. V. (2010). *The Fluent Reader* (2nd ed.). New York: Scholastic.

Rasinski, T., & Hamman, P. (2010). Fluency—why it is not hot. *Reading Today,* August/September (26).

Rasinski, T., & Padak, N. (2007). *Effective reading strategies: Teaching children who find reading difficult.* Upper Saddle River, NJ: Pearson.

Rasinski, T., Padak, N, Newton, R. M, & Newton, E. (2008). *Greek and Latin roots: Keys to building vocabulary.* Huntington Beach, CA: Shell Education.

Rogers, L. (1999). Spelling cheerleading. *The Reading Teacher, 53*(2), 110–111.

Smith, K. (2008). *How to be an explorer of the world.* New York: Penguin.

Stahl, S. A., & Fairbanks, M. M. (1986). The effects of vocabulary instruction: A model-based meta-analysis. *Review of Educational Research, 56*(1), 72–110.

Winters, R. (2001). Vocabulary anchors: Building conceptual connections with young readers. *The Reading Teacher, 54*(7), 659–662.

Yopp, R. H., & Yopp, H. K. (2007). Ten important words plus: A strategy for building word knowledge. *The Reading Teacher, 61,* 157–160.

Zarry, L. (1999). Vocabulary enrichment in composition. *Education, 120,* 267–271.

Name _____   Date _____

Vocabulary Anchor

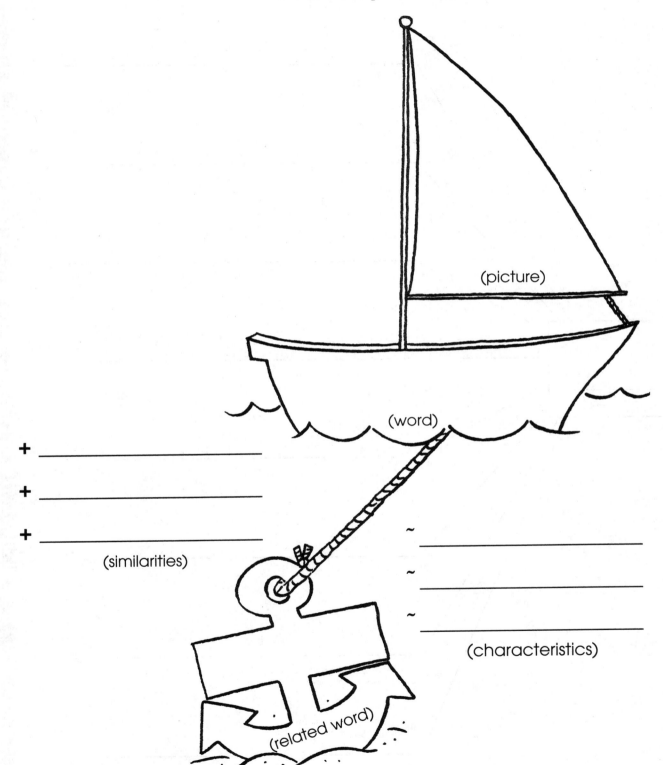

(picture)

(word)

+ _____

+ _____

+ _____

(similarities)

~ _____

~ _____

~ _____

(characteristics)

(related word)

Prefix "Splash"

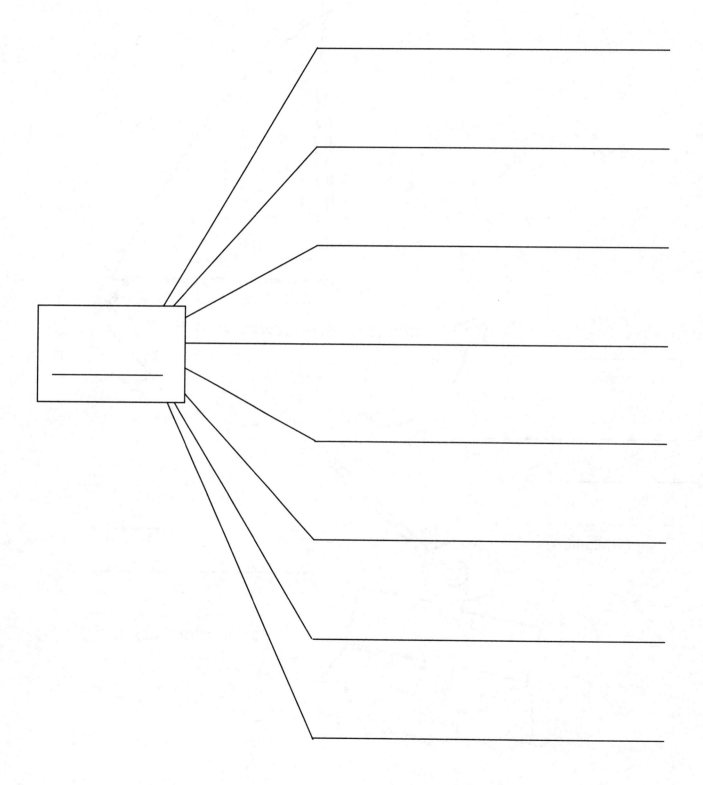

The Next Step in Vocabulary Instruction © 2012 by Karen Bromley, Scholastic Teaching Resources

Word Wheel

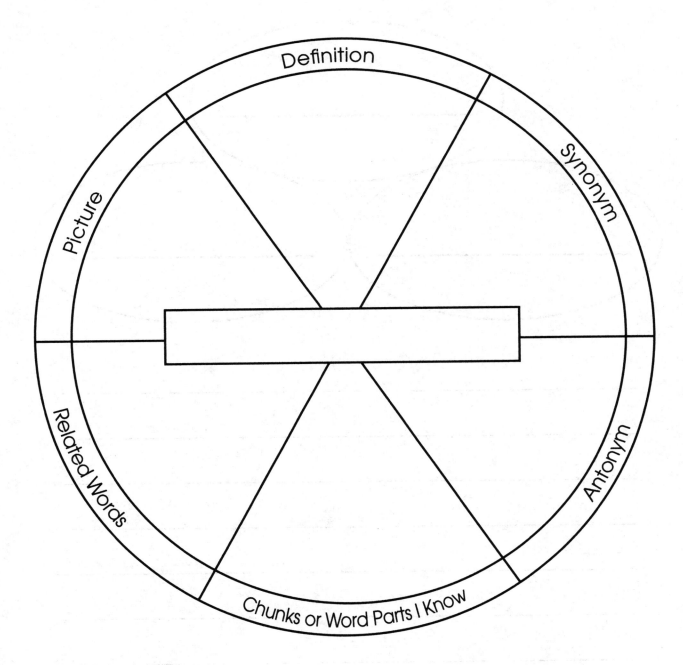

"Key" Word Summary

_____

_____

_____

_____

_____

_____

_____

_____

 The Next Step in Vocabulary Instruction © 2012 by Karen Bromley, Scholastic Teaching Resources

Name _____ Date _____

"Magnet" Words

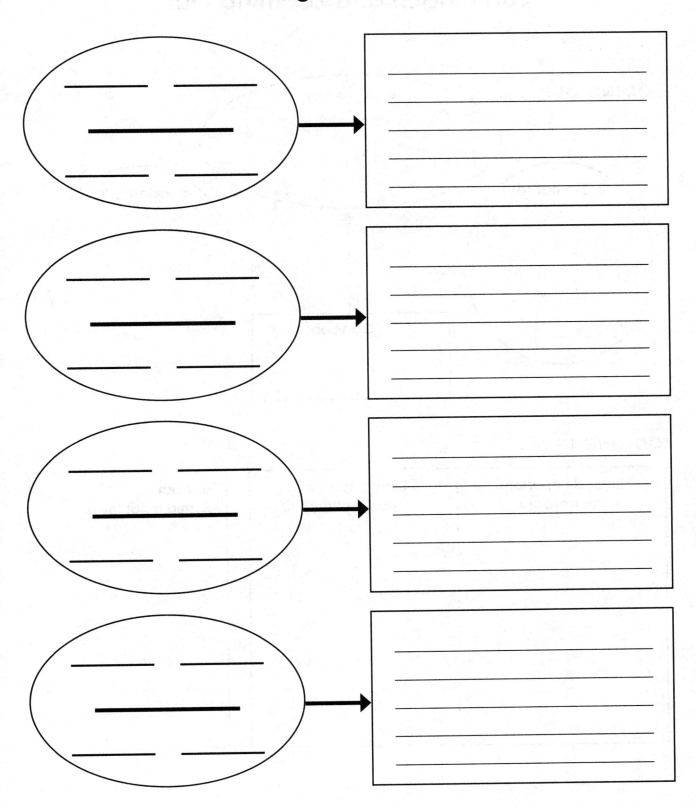

Zooming In and Zooming Out

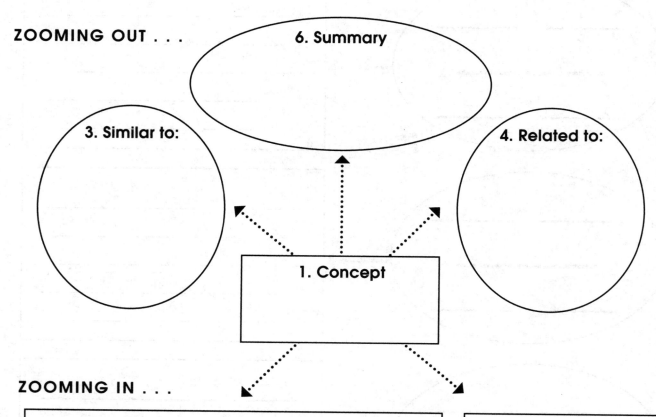

ZOOMING OUT . . .

6. Summary

3. Similar to:

4. Related to:

1. Concept

ZOOMING IN . . .

| 2. Most important information: | Least important information: | 5. What _____ might not tell us: |

The Next Step in Vocabulary Instruction © 2012 by Karen Bromley, Scholastic Teaching Resources

Word Ladder

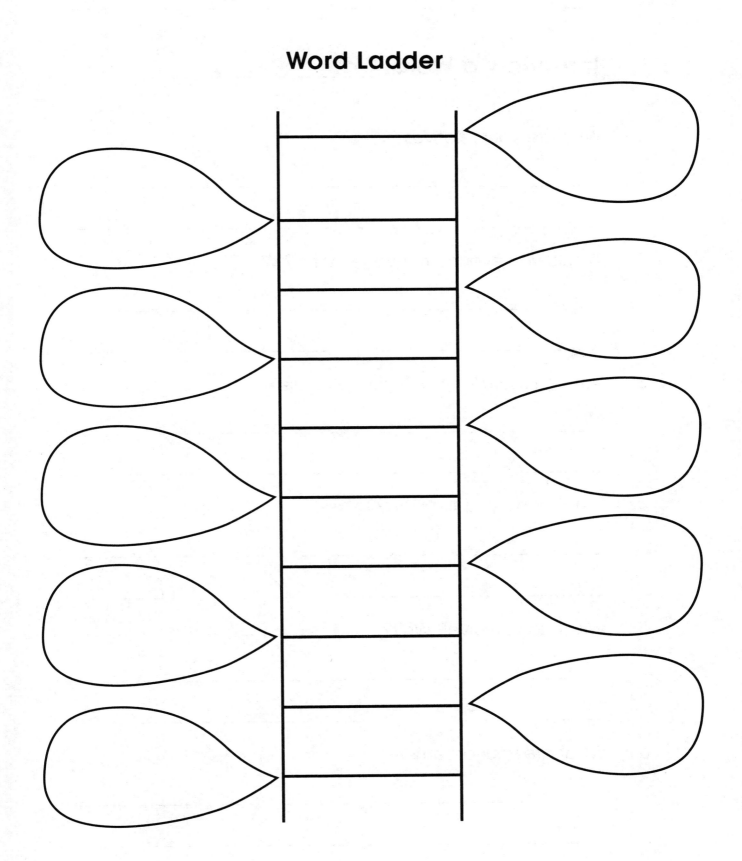

Names _____ Date _____

Interview a Word: _____

 1 Who are your relatives?

_____

_____

 2 Would you ever hurt anyone? Who? Why?

_____

_____

 3 Are you useful? What is your purpose?

_____

_____

 4 What don't you like? Why?

_____

_____

 5 What do you love? Why?

_____

_____

 6 What are your dreams?

_____

_____

The Next Step in Vocabulary Instruction © 2012 by Karen Bromley, Scholastic Teaching Resources